This book is dedicated to Hele
without whom it — and life itself — v

— The Henry family

# *A Few of Our* Favorite Meals..................2
Helen's best dishes as judged by her children

# Family Specialties.....................14
Food used to raise two generations

# New Additions............48
Third generation contributions

On the cover:
Strawberry Cake, page 39

Photography: Steve and Tiffany Warmowski of Warmowski Photography
and Brian and Lori Everett
Design and editing: Heather Seely
Food prep: Colleen Cooksey

# A Few of Our Favorite Meals

## MIKE HENRY

*Growing up, I always looked forward to mealtime. Besides having a big appetite and a Mom who was a great cook, I also had four sisters who ate like birds to stay slim and trim. That meant I was the "clean up" guy. No, not as in baseball, but as in "Mike, finish up all of the leftovers." Or "Mike, do you think you could clean up your sisters' plates?" Of course, the answer was always a resounding, "Yes!" However, when it came to dessert, the girls did me no such favors as we all loved those home made desserts that magically appeared at every meal. And we haven't changed a bit over the years with regard to the Henry version of the "main course."*

*Naturally, I married a woman who rarely ate dessert as a kid and who has carried on that tradition to the present and undoubtedly foreseeable future. (However, she has neat assets that offset this one "minor" liability.) So just before we come down for a visit when Mom says, "Mike, what kind of pie do you want this time?" it's like music to my ears. And when we have a group get together, complete with lots of varieties of desserts, it's like a whole symphony orchestra exploding with beautiful music.*

*What are my favorite desserts? That's a tough one. If I had to narrow it down to five, it would be four different types of pie (butterscotch, lemon, cherry, and pecan) and meringue cookie squares (the ones with the chocolate chips and nuts). And I shouldn't leave out sheet cake with caramel icing. Mmm, my mouth is watering just thinking about all of these goodies!*

When I first met the Henrys over 40 years ago, I was amazed at the amount of wonderful desserts that were served for dinner each day. I also loved all the different kinds of food that Grandma Henry cooked. Not only did she cook for a large family, but also anyone who happened to be around was invited to sit down to dinner. Since many of the same faces showed up quite often at dinner time, I think some of the kids' friends made it a point to be around at dinner time!

Most everything that I served my own family over the years came from Grandma Henry's recipes. When I told Laura that recipes were being collected for this book, she said that most of the recipes she uses are also from Grandma Henry. One of the Henry recipes became not only a favorite but also a tradition in my parents' home and that of my brothers. It's our very most favorite ham loaf served with what we call pineapple goop (another Henry recipe). For many years this has been our traditional Christmas Eve dinner. My family, the Even family, always gathered in Florida for Christmas each year, but we never seemed to remember to bring the ham loaf recipe with us. Thus, we would need to make an annual call to Grandma Henry for the recipe. Then we would all argue that she changed the recipe each year! Our Christmas Eve dinner always turned out to be what we thought was the best meal of the holiday season. My brothers and my family still look forward to this Christmas Eve meal! Not a Christmas Eve goes by that we don't relish this favorite meal and reminisce about all of the wonderful meals enjoyed at the Henry home.

I have never been able to duplicate all of the many yummy desserts served at the Henry home with each meal. It still amazes me to see, all these years later, the table loaded with so many delicious tasting goodies. Her pecan pie is my personal favorite. I think all of the desserts are Mike's favorites. As we travel to Grandma's house, we love to anticipate what dessert will be served on this particular trip. No matter what Grandma selects to serve, we know it will be absolutely scrumptious. And the best part of all is that no one is a more loving hostess than Grandma Henry!

— Jeanne Henry

## Ham Loaf

Have the butcher mix: 1 1/2 lb ham meat and 1 lb pork. Add to meat: 1 egg, 1/2 cup milk, 1 cup fine cracker crumbs, 1 T horseradish, 1 tsp onion, pepper, Lawry's season salt. Mix together and shape into a loaf. Place on baking sheet and bake at 350 for 1 1/2 hours. You may baste with a brown sugar, vinegar, water, mustard mixture.

## Scalloped Pineapple

2 1/2 cups crushed pineapple
1 cup pineapple juice
1 cup sugar
2 T. flour
1/2 cup butter
Cook all the above until thick.
Place 4 slices of bread which has been cubed in a greased 8" X 8" pan and pour the above mixture over the top. Bake at 350 degrees for 30 minutes

## Butterscotch Pie

1 1/2 cups of brown sugar
3 T. cornstarch
3 T. flour
pinch of salt
Mix the above, then add:
2 1/4 cups of evp. milk (1/2 evp. milk and 1/2 water)  NO SUBSTITUTIONS
3 egg yolks, beat
Mix well, then cook until thick. Let cool. Then add 3 T. butter and 1 1/2 t. vanilla
Pour into cooked pie shell and top with meringue. Cook as directed for meringue.

## Pat Pinkerton

*My mom was a great cook. When I was growing up we always had home-cooked meals, partly to save money for a family of six kids and partly because we grew up in a small town that didn't have many restaurants, and people didn't eat out often – once a week at the most. So, I continued the tradition while raising my four kids. We always had a hot breakfast whether it was scrambled eggs or French toast with an occasional treat like bacon or ham on Sundays. Sunday mornings I was up early and baked homemade cinnamon or pecan rolls. It wasn't always easy to do, especially with a budget of $10 a week for food in the early sixties. I worked in dessert at least once a day – with four kids it disappeared by nightfall. When I started going with my husband, Bob, his friend who knew my family better than he did, warned him gravely that my family "loved their desserts." When Bob told me this months later I thought, "If that's the worst that his friend could think of, I guess we're ok." Bob and I have been happily married for over 20 years. Now he looks for a little something sweet at the end of each meal.*

I have heard many cynics say that life in the fifties wasn't like *Father Knows Best* or *Leave It To Beaver*. But, luckily, it was for some of us. In a small town in central Illinois it was very much like those shows for my family. My father had a business and my mother was a stay-at-home mom. Both my parents worked hard — my dad who had to be skilled in all aspects of a small mill business and my mother in caring for six children. Back in the old days we walked home from school for lunch every day. There was always something hot and good waiting for us. Supper was even better. After a busy day at school, one of the things to look forward to was a big supper. We all started hanging around the kitchen when Mom was preparing it, hoping that she would cook one of our favorites. Actually everything that she cooked was our favorite. Mealtime was bustling with conversation about each person's day. I think at the time we took it for granted that the meals were deliciously prepared. Later, when we four girls were older, we all learned to cook in Mom's kitchen. And we all still love to cook, especially for our families. This cookbook is only a sample of the many meals and warm memories that we all have carried with us and passed on to our children.

### Stuffed Pork Chops

8 1-1/2 inch thick, center cut Pork Chops
2 Cups Breadcrumbs
1/2 Cup Celery, finely chopped
1/2 Cup Onions, finely chopped
1/4 Cup Parsley
1 Teaspoon Poultry Seasoning
1/2 Teaspoon Salt
Milk

Have butcher cut a pocket in the chops.
Combine the ingredients for the stuffing (breadcrumbs, celery, onions, parsley, poultry seasoning and salt). Add milk to moisten. Fill the pockets with the stuffing. (You may need to skewer the chops with toothpicks to keep the stuffing in.) Brown the chops on both sides in a hot skillet that has been sprayed with non-stick coating. Place the browned chops in a large baking dish. Pour milk into the pan, lifting the chops so that it covers the bottom. Cover and cook at 350 for 1 to 1 1/2 hours or until the chops are spoon tender. Note: "Stove Top" stuffing could be used in this recipe.

## AUGRATIN POTATOES

Place a layer of sliced, peeled red potatoes in a baking pan. Sprinkle with a little flour, salt, pepper, garlic salt, finely chopped onion and chunks of Velveeta. Keep layering another time or two. Pour milk in to just below the top of the last layer of potatoes. Bake at 350 for 1 hour. You can vary the size of your dish, depending upon how many you are serving. An 8 X 8 pan works for up to 4, a 9 X 12 pan for 8 to 10.

## CREAM PIE — COCONUT, CHOCOLATE OR BANANA

1 3/4 cups milk
1/4 cup white Karo Syrup
Scald

1/4 cup milk
4 T. cornstarch
Mix
1/2 cup sugar
pinch salt
Add to cornstarch mixture

Beat 3 egg yolks. Add to cornstarch mixture.
Add mixture to scalded milk. Cook and stir until thick. Cover and cook 5 more minutes. Cool and add 1 t. vanilla.
To make banana pie, cool above mixture and line baked pie shell with bananas and top with whipped cream or meringue.
To make chocolate pie, use 1 cup sugar and 2 oz. unsweetened chocolate. Add before cooking.
To make coconut, add 3/4 cup coconut to cooked filling and top meringue with coconut before cooking.
To make graham cracker pie, add basic cream pie to a graham cracker crust, top with meringue.

## Colleen Cooksey

*Mom was always called upon to fix things for bake sales. Her divinity was her signature item. Another recipe she made frequently were the pecan surprise squares. We all remember how she would take the good, soft parts to the bake sale, and we got the crusty outside. I still make myself sick on these when I make them because I am so excited to get to eat the inside pieces too!*

*Her pies are to die for. It took at least two to serve us all.*

*To this day, the majority of the recipes in my files originate with Mom. You do need to be careful though because sometimes she changes them around, thus, yours will never taste as good as hers.*

I am a firm believer in the importance of family meals. That belief comes from our childhood. My mind is full of pleasant memories of the good times we had sharing the delicious meals Mom cooked daily.

I feel like we were blessed to have a "June Cleaver" mother. No she didn't dress in heels and pearls, but she was always there for us when we got home from school most likely in the kitchen preparing a special dessert to go with supper. Many meals we didn't just have a dessert but a choice of desserts most of which were homemade. Yes, we have a sweet tooth.

I started cooking somewhere around age 10 when I joined 4-H. Mom was always patient with me as I tried the recipes for whatever level I was at. She would be there to help but made sure I did the work. How else could I learn? And of course she made sure I cleaned up after myself.

We all share memories of certain meals she fixed, but her meals were anything but routine as she loved to try new recipes. This is a love she has to this day.

### Swiss Steak

1 can stewed tomatoes with onions, celery and green peppers
2 beef cubed steaks
1/2 cup flour
1/2 teaspoon Lawry's Seasoned Salt
salt and pepper to taste
shortening or oil

In a large skillet, melt shortening. Meanwhile combine the flour and seasonings. Dip steaks in seasoned flour mixture and brown in hot grease. Turn and brown on other side. Cover with tomatoes. Cover skillet and simmer for an hour. Yield: 2 servings

### Boiled potatoes

Peel and cube desired amount of potatoes. (I prefer white but Mom usually used red.) Place into boiling, salted water. Cook for 15-20 minutes depending upon size of cubes. Drain. Add butter and seasoning if desired.

## Pecan Surprise Squares

1/2 cup shortening
1 cup sugar
2 eggs
1 teaspoon vanilla
2 cups sifted flour
1 teaspoon baking powder
1 teaspoon salt
7 oz chocolate chips
Topping:
3 egg whites
1 1/2 cups brown sugar
1/2 cup chopped pecans

Cream thoroughly the shortening and white sugar. Add eggs and vanilla and beat until fluffy. Sift the dry ingredients together. Stir into creamed mixture. Spread in 8 x 12" pan. Bake at 350 for 10 minutes. Meanwhile make a meringue by beating the egg whites until slightly stiff then beating in the brown sugar. Beat until stiff. Sprinkle the cooked crust with chocolate chips. Top with meringue spreading to seal to the side of the pan. Sprinkle with chopped nuts. Cook for 10 additional minutes or until golden brown.

## Nancy Rhoades

*I suppose growing up I took Mom's home-cooked meals for granted. I thought everyone came home from school to a house filled with the delectable smells of supper being prepared. What I do remember is an instant and complete transformation of my mood, from burned-out brain to anticipation of airing all of my day's complaints and accomplishments while sharing a delicious family meal. The only disappointment I ever had was if the "only" dessert was ice cream! Gee, Mom, no pie?!!*

*While raising our four sons, I used all of Mom's recipes and have shared many of them with my daughters-in-law.*

It's funny how shuffling through old recipes can bring back memories. I chose "Chipper Chicken" because it reminded me of when I was dating my husband Marty. It was one of his favorites, and I liked to "show off" my cooking abilities for him. When we were newly married, I made it quite often for the same reason and because a whole chicken was only about $2.00 and we were on a tight budget.

### Chipper Chicken

1 medium bag potato chips
1/4 cup butter
1 tsp. garlic salt
1 tsp. salt
1/8 tsp. pepper
2-3 lb. chicken, cut in pieces (or use boneless breasts)

Heat oven to 350 degrees. Crush chips finely. Melt butter in pan and add seasonings. Roll chicken in seasoned butter, then in chips. Place in oblong pan (9X13X2). Bake 1 and 1/4 hours (30 minutes for boneless breasts).

### Mashed Potatoes

Peel and cut up potatoes. Cover with water, salt, and boil until tender. Drain. Add one tbl. butter per potato and mash. Add milk until a little thinner than desired. (They will thicken upon standing.) Add other seasonings (salt, pepper, season salt) as desired. Finally, add one tbl. of sour cream for each potato.

### Layered Green Beans

1 can french-style green beans
1 small can water chestnuts (optional)
1 can cream of mushroom soup
Parmesan or velveeta cheese

In casserole dish, repeat above layering. Bake 20 minutes 350 degrees.
Top with canned onion rings. Bake 10 more minutes.

## APPLE CRISP

5-6 cups peeled and sliced apples (I prefer Jonathans)
Place apples in over-sized pie plate or 6X10 pan.

Mix together until crumbly and sprinkle over apples:
1 cup flour
1/2 to 1 cup sugar
1 tsp. baking powder
3/4 tsp salt
1 unbeaten egg

Pour over above:
3/4 stick margarine
1/2 tsp. cinnamon, dash nutmeg

Bake 350 degrees for 30-40 minutes

## Maureen Agner

Chinese New Year Cookies were a favorite of Danny and mine. Mom would set them up in the fridge on the back porch of the North Cain house. Danny and I would always get excited when she would head for the back porch after supper because we knew she would walk back carrying a wax-paper covered cookie sheet with mounds of these crunchy, chocolate cookies.

Brunches were a time when guests or visiting family members were present to share in a casual, relaxed meal. On the menu was sausage patties, egg casserole, homemade waffles with warm maple syrup and butter that was kept warm and melted in a special candle-lit server.

### Waffles

2 eggs
2 cups buttermilk (this recipe must have real buttermilk)
1/3 cup vegetable oil
2 cups all-purpose flour
1 teaspoon soda
2 teaspoons baking powder
1/2 teaspoon salt

Heat waffle iron while preparing batter. Beat eggs well. Stir in buttermilk and oil. Sift together the flour, soda, powder and salt. Combine with liquids stirring with a wire whisk until mixed. Pour batter onto hot waffle iron using the amount specified by the manufacturer. Cook until brown.

### Homemade Maple Syrup

2 cups sugar
1 cup water
Bring to a boil and cook to dissolve sugar. Add 1 tsp maple flavoring.

### Banana Salad

1 can pineapple tidbits (reserve 1/2 cup juice)
1 egg beaten
1 T sugar
2 T flour
4 large marshmallows
1 cup mini marshmallows
sliced bananas

Cook juice, egg, sugar, flour, and marshmallow until thick. Add pineapple, miniature marshmallows, sliced bananas and pecan pieces if desired.

## Egg Casserole

(You can make the night ahead.)
5 slices buttered bread cut in 1/2" cubes
4 eggs, beaten
2 cups milk
1/2 lb shredded cheddar cheese
salt/pepper to taste
Any combination of meat or veggies can be added such as sausage, ham, green pepper, mushrooms, onions.
Mix all ingredients together and pour into casserole dish. Let stand at least one hour. Bake at 350 for one hour. (Check after 45 minutes. Aluminum foil may be needed to protect from over-browning.)

## Dan Henry

*I have so many fond memories of mom's cooking, I can't narrow it down to a particular story. Ham Loaf, Chipper Chicken, and Ham, Green Bean and Potato Caserole from holidays and special occasions; Ice Cream with Homemade Hot Fudge Sauce, Wacky Cake, and Strawberry Cake for dessert; trimmings from the edges of bar cookies that mom made for Bridge Club. So many great memories of food shared (and fought over) with our large, wonderful family. I'm lucky I still weigh under 185 pounds after Mom's great cooking and having all of my wife Jessica's delicious food over the years. I was lucky enough to find a woman so much like my mother in many ways, especially the talent of preparing delicious dishes.*

I never have been much of a cook. The only things that really stand out in my limited experience are homemade caramel and lasagna. The homemade caramel goes back to my early teen years. I think the recipe must have been next to another popular one in the Betty Crocker Cookbook, and I guess I noticed it when mom was making divinity or something. It sounded so delicious, and Mom talked me into making it myself. I remember making it several times, and it seems like it turned out pretty good each time. I also remember people marveling that it turned out so good, and I couldn't understand why. I just thought they were humoring me. It was a pretty simple recipe, along the lines of non-fattening items like sugar, butter, cream, and probably some vanilla. (Sorry I can't remember the exact recipe.) I guess the key was cooking it the right amount of time at the right temperature. That's the part I must have done right. I remember getting brave one time and adding melted Hershey bars on the top, and Aunt Kate just raved about it.

The lasagna was my most ambitious undertaking, especially considering I didn't have the confidence to do even grilled cheese by myself. I made it for my beautiful wife Jessica's birthday when we were both in our early twenties. I was a little nervous about it turning out well. I can't remember if she gave me any help or not; probably at minimum some moral support. She said it was delicious, so I guess I did all right. I really haven't done anything that involved ever since. It made me appreciate all of the work that goes into a meal, and Jessie has made so many great ones for us over the years. I try to at least help with the dishes and shopping. That's the parts I know I can handle.

### Ham and Potato Casserole

1/4 cup butter
teaspoon chopped onion, if desired
1/4 cup flour
2 cups milk
1 cup American cheese
dash salt, pepper
2 cups cooked, sliced potatoes
1 can green beans, drained

2 cups (or more) diced ham
1 1/2 cups buttered bread crumbs

Make cheese sauce by melting butter in skillet. Cook onion in butter, if desired. Stir in flour. Using a wire whisk, slowly stir in milk and cook while stirring until thick. Add cheese and cook until melted. Add seasoning. Place drained potatoes in a 2-quart casserole dish that has been sprayed with non-stick coating. Top with green beans. Pour half of cheese sauce over. Top with ham then remaining cheese sauce. End with buttered bread crumbs. Bake at 350 for 30-35 minutes.

## Banana Bread

1 3/4 cups flour
2 teaspoons baking powder
1/2 teaspoon salt
1/4 teaspoon baking soda
1/3 cup shortening
2/3 cup sugar
2 eggs
1 cup mashed bananas

Mix together the dry ingredients and set aside. Cream shortening with sugar until creamy.
Add eggs one at a time. Add 1/4 of the flour mixture alternating with the bananas. After each addition, beat until smooth. Pour batter into a greased loaf pan. Bake at 350 for 1 hour.

# Family Specialties
## Food used to raise two generations

### Cottage Cheese Fluff Salad
*Helen*

1 (3 oz.) package Jello, flavor of choice (Mom did orange normally)
1 can crushed pineapple in its own juice
1 (8 oz.) container cottage cheese, small curd
1 (8 oz.) container Cool Whip

In a large mixing bowl, stir Jello into pineapple until dissolved. Stir in cottage cheese. Fold in whipped topping. Chill.

### Asiago Potato Puffs
*Jeanne, daughter-in-law*
(These are so good for an appetizer)

15-20 petite red-skinned potatoes (halved lengthwise)

Mix the following:
1 cup mayo. (The real stuff works best.)
1 cup finely grated Asiago cheese
6 cloves of garlic minced (more to taste)
1/2 teaspoon each of white pepper and salt

Trim the bottom of potatoes so they lay flat. Hollow out middle of each half. Blanch 2-3 minutes in boiling water and immediately drop in ice water. Drain and cool. Fill with the above mixture. Broil 2 to 3 minutes until golden.

## *Tales from the Kitchen*

Agner's advice to their children: Eat as a family around a table – no TV. This became more of a challenge as the kids and their activities grew, but we always managed this several times a week.

**Maureen, daughter**

## Spinach Balls
*Helen*

3 10 Ounce Packages Frozen, Chopped Spinach, cooked and well drained
1 Cup Butter or Margarine, melted
3/4 Teaspoon Salt
1 Package Stove Top Dressing Mix
6 Large Eggs, beaten
1 Small Onion, chopped finely
1 1/2 Cups Parmesan Cheese, grated
2 Cups Bisquick

In large mixing bowl, combine all ingredients. Form into small balls (teaspoon size). Place on waxed paper on cookie sheet. Freeze. To store frozen for a period of time, place in covered container. Cook at 350 for 20-30 minutes or until lightly browned.

**Tips and Tricks**
Work with your ingredients (eggs, meat, etc.) at room temperature unless recipe states otherwise.
*Maureen, daughter*

## Cheese Fondue Appetizers
*Colleen, daughter*

1 Jar Old English Cheese Spread
1 Stick Butter or Margarine
1 Egg
1 Loaf French Bread, cut into cubes

Microwave the cheese and butter on medium until cheese is softened and butter is melted. Stir in egg until blended. Dip bread cubes one at a time in the cheese mixture. Place on cookie sheet that has been sprayed with non-stick coating. Bake at 350 for 8-10 minutes. To make ahead: place dipped, uncooked cubes on wax paper on cookie sheet and freeze. When frozen, store in covered container. Bake as directed when ready to use.

## Rye Bread Dip
*Maureen, daughter*

1 1/3 Cups Salad Dressing (Miracle Whip)
1 1/3 Cups Sour Cream
2 Tablespoons Parsley Flakes
2 Tablespoons Minced Onion
2 Teaspoons Beau Monde Seasoning
2 Teaspoons Dill Weed
1 Loaf Round Rye Bread

Mix all ingredients together except rye bread. Chill. To serve, cut off the top of the loaf or bread to make a "bowl" for the dip. Break the bread into bite size pieces. Fill "bowl" with dip. This is also good served with vegetables also.

## Shrimp Snack
*Colleen, daughter*

8 Ounces Cooked Small Shrimp
8 Ounces Cream Cheese, softened
1 Tablespoon Worcestershire Sauce
1 Jar Cocktail Sauce

In small mixing bowl, combine softened cream cheese and Worcestershire sauce. Spread in thin layer on round tray or plate to cover approximately 10". Top with cocktail sauce. Carefully top with the shrimp. Chill. To serve: spread on snack crackers.

Shrimp Snack

CRAB MEAT DELIGHTS

### CRAB MEAT DELIGHTS
*Jessie, daughter-in-law*

1 (6 or 7 oz.) can crab meat, drained
1/2 stick butter, softened
1/2 stick margarine, softened
1 (15 oz.) jar Old English Cheese Spread
1 1/2 teaspoons mayonnaise
1/2 teaspoon garlic salt
6 English muffins

Mix ingredients except the muffins together. Spread on halves of muffins. Bake or broil until brown.

### SAUSAGE BALLS
*Jessie, daughter-in-law*

2 cups baking mix
1 lb. sausage
10 oz. shredded cheddar cheese

Combine all ingredients and shape into small balls. Bake at 350 for 15 minutes.

### MOM'S ROLLS
*Nancy, daughter*

(36-40 roles or 15 rolls and one 9X12 pan of cinnamon rolls)
Melt: 3/4 cup Butter Crisco in microwave
Add: 1 cup sugar
     2 cups lukewarm water
Add: 2 pkg. yeast (dissolve)
Add: 2 eggs, beaten
     1 tsp. salt
Add: 7 cups flour. Use dough hooks on mixer and mix until it is smooth and not sticky (may have to add a little more flour)
Cover. Let rise overnight in refrigerator or 2-3 hours at room temperature.
Roll out 1/2 inch thick. Use 3-inch round cutter to cut circles. Place on greased cookie sheet. Put pad of butter on each and fold over. Let rise.
Bake at 350 degrees for 12-15 minutes on top shelf. Butter on top when hot.
To make cinnamon rolls:
Melt 1/2 stick butter and spread over rolled out doe. Sprinkle with cinnamon sugar until covered . Roll up tightly. Cut 3/4 inch slices. Bake 15-20 min., 350 degrees in greased 9X12. Ice with butter cream frosting (butter, powdered sugar, vanilla, milk).

### EASY DONUTS
*Colleen, daughter*

1 can refrigerated Biscuits
Shortening for frying
2 Tablespoons Milk
1/2 Cup Powdered Sugar
1 Teaspoon Vanilla

Heat 1" shortening in electric skillet to 350. Meanwhile remove the biscuits from the can and separate. Using a donut hole cutter, make a hole in the middle of each. Fry the holes turning when one side is brown. Place on paper towels to drain. Continue frying a few donuts at a time. Prepare glaze with milk, powdered sugar and vanilla. Dip donuts in glaze, coating both sides.

> *"Edie Mc Collister first introduced me to this bread recipe which makes a delicious, slightly sweet and buttery dinner roll as well as perfect cinnamon rolls. Now, my children call them "Mom's Rolls," the fastest way to my daughter-in-laws' hearts!"*
>
> **Nancy, daughter**

MOM'S ROLLS

## Donut Balls
*Colleen, daughter*

2 Cups Bisquick Baking Mix (either regular or low fat will work)
2 Tablespoons Sugar
1 Teaspoon Vanilla
1 Egg, slightly beaten
1/4 Cup Milk
1 Teaspoon Cinnamon
1/2 Teaspoon Nutmeg
Powdered Sugar

Heat shortening in skillet to 350. Using a wire whip, combine egg, vanilla and milk in medium mixing bowl. Add bisquick, sugar, cinnamon, and nutmeg. Mix until ingredients are combined. (Batter will be thick.) Drop by teaspoonfuls into hot grease. (Tip: to drop balls easier, heat a teaspoon in the grease before using it to dip batter. Then the batter will come off the spoon with ease.) Fry on each side until brown. Drain on paper towels. Shake in bag with powdered sugar. Serve immediately. If you have any left-over, they can successfully be re-heated in the microwave. Yield: 4 dozen.

**Easy Donuts**

## Blueberry Muffins
*Jessie, daughter-in-law*

Batter:
1 1/2 cups flour
3/4 cup sugar
1/2 teaspoon salt
2 teaspoons baking powder
1/3 cup oil
1 egg
1/3 cup milk
1 cup fresh or frozen blueberries
Streusel:
1/2 cup sugar
1/3 cup flour
1/4 cup butter, cubed
1 1/2 teaspoons cinnamon

Combine flour, sugar, salt and baking powder. Mix oil, egg and milk together then add to dry ingredients. Fold in blueberries. Mixture will be stiff. Fill muffin cups up to the top. Mix streusel ingredients together until crumbly and sprinkle over muffins. Bake at 400 for 20-25 minutes.

*"Easy Donuts were first shared with us by an old boyfriend of mine. He is long gone, but the recipe lives on."*

**Colleen, daughter**

**Blueberry Muffins**

## CHEESE GARLIC BREADSTICKS
*Jessie, daughter-in-law*

1 3/4 to 2 1/2 cups flour
1 pkg. active dry yeast
1/2 teaspoon salt
1 cup water
3 tablespoons oil, divided
1 tablespoon honey
2 tablespoons Italian seasonings
1 teaspoon garlic salt
1/2 cup shredded mozzarella
1/2 cup grated Parmesan cheese

Combine 1 1/2 cups flour, yeast and salt. In saucepan, heat water, honey and 1 tablespoon oil to 120 degrees. Add to dry ingredients and beat until just moistened. Stir in enough remaining flour to form a soft dough. Turn onto a lightly floured surface and knead until smooth and elastic. Cover and let rest 15 minutes. Grease a 15 x10" baking sheet. Roll dough into a 15 x 10" rectangle. Transfer to baking sheet. Press dough to edges. Brush with remaining oil. Sprinkle with seasonings and garlic salt. Cover and let rise 40 minutes. Bake in a preheated oven at 400 for 10 minutes. Sprinkle with cheeses and bake 3-5 minutes longer. Serve warm cut into strips.

## BEER BATTER BREAD
*Jessie, daughter-in-law*

2 1/2 cups flour
2 tablespoons sugar
1/2 teaspoon salt
1 pkg. active dry yeast
1 cup beer
1 tablespoon butter
1 tablespoon honey
1 egg

Combine flour, sugar, salt and yeast and mix to blend. In small saucepan, combine beer, butter and honey and heat to very warm. Pour into flour mixture then mix in the egg. Beat at medium speed for 3 minutes. Cover and let rise 30 minutes. Stir down dough and pour into a greased and floured loaf pan. Cover and let rise 15 minutes then bake in a preheated oven at 375 for 30-35 minutes.

## Tales from the Kitchen

When the kids were growing up, each week or two we would get out the board games and have a family game night. I always made chocolate chip cookies. In fact, you can tell the most popular games by the amount of chocolate smeared on them. (Clue wins.)

**Maureen, daughter**

## Grasshoppers
*Colleen, daughter*

1 Quart Soft Serve Ice Cream
2 Ounces (1/4 Cup) Creme de Menthe (green)
2 Ounces (1/4 Cup) Creme de Cacao (white)

In blender combine ingredients and blend until smooth. Pour into small serving glasses or freeze for serving later.

## Champagne Punch
*Colleen, daughter*

2 bottles champagne
1 bottle Chablis
1/2 bottle ginger ale
1 bag frozen whole strawberries, unsweetened

Slowly pour liquids into punch bowl. Add strawberries. Serve immediately. The strawberries keep the punch cold and add flavor.

## Egg and Tuna Scallop
*Helen*

2 tablespoons butter
2 tablespoons flour
1 cup milk
1/4 teaspoon salt
dash pepper
1 tablespoon onion
1 (3 oz.) can tuna in water, drained
4 hard boiled eggs, sliced
2 cups crushed potato chips

Make a white sauce by melting the butter in a pan. Stir in flour using a wire whisk. Slowly add milk and cook until thickened. Add seasonings including onion. Put half of potato chips into 1 1/2 quart casserole which has been sprayed with non-stick coating. Next arrange layer of tuna then sliced eggs. Pour white sauce over all. Top with remaining chips. Bake at 375 for 30 minutes.

**Tips and Tricks**
Pull a chair up to the counter and let your kids cook with you

**Maureen, daughter**

## Salmon Patties
*Helen*

1 can salmon, drained and bones removed
1 egg, beaten
1/4 cup milk
1/4 cup cracker crumbs
1 tablespoon minced onion
dash pepper
oil for cooking

Combine milk and egg. Stir in remaining ingredients. Form into patties. Fry in hot (350) oil until brown and turn to cook on other side.

**Beer Batter Bread**

HAMBURGER STEAKS

ITALIAN BEEF

> "When the girls were young and I would go out, Hamburger Hash was always the meal I made to leave with the babysitter. It was quick, easy, and well-balanced."
>
> **Colleen, daughter**

HAMBURGER HASH

### HAMBURGER STEAKS
*Colleen, daughter*

1 1/2 pounds lean ground chuck
2 Eggs, beaten slightly
1/4 Cup Catsup
2 Tablespoons Worcestershire Sauce
2 Tablespoons Prepared Mustard
2 Tablespoons A1 Steak Sauce
1/2 Teaspoon Lowry's Season Salt
1/4 Teaspoon Pepper
2 Dashes Salt

Combine all ingredients except hamburger in large bowl. Add hamburger and mix. Shape into 6 patties. Cook over hot coals for 10 minutes. Turn and cook an additional 8-10 minutes or until done. Avoid flattening the burgers with a spatula as this will decrease the juiciness. Note: Cook until done due to the presence of the eggs.

### MEAT LOAF
*Colleen, daughter*

Use above ingredients except A1. Add one to two slices of bread, cubed or 5 crackers, crushed. Shape into a loaf in a greased bread pan. Or you can bake it on a cookie sheet in shape of loaf. Bake at 350 for an hour. Pour off grease. Slice and serve. Yield: 4-6 servings. Note: To make a smaller loaf, just reduce ingredients. For instance, for one pound of ground beef, I use only 1 egg. This is not an exact measure. I actually just shake all stuff in.

### ITALIAN BEEF
*Pat, daughter*

2 to 3 pound beef roast — sprinkle with garlic powder, basil, oregano and pepper
Place in slow cooker
Add 1/2 cup water, 1/2 cup peppercini juice, 1/4 bottle fennel
Cook for at least 3 hours. Remove meat, shred and return to crock pot and keep warm until served.

### HAMBURGER HASH
*Helen*

1 Tablespoon Chopped Onion
1/2 Pound Lean Ground Beef
2 Potatoes, peeled and cubed
2 large carrots, peeled and sliced (or peeled baby carrots)
1 Tablespoon Beef Bouillon
2 Tablespoons Cornstarch
Salt and Pepper to taste
Season salt
Dash Accent
1 Tablespoon Kitchen Bouquet

Brown hamburger and onion in saucepan. Drain grease and return hamburger to saucepan. Add potatoes, carrots, 1/2 cup water and bouillon. Simmer until carrots are soft (10 minutes). Prepare a paste with cornstarch and 1/4 cup water. Stir into cooked mixture. Cook until thickened. Add seasonings and Kitchen Bouquet. Yield: 2 servings.

## MADE RITE
*Helen*

1-1 1/2 pounds ground beef
salt and pepper
garlic powder
onion flakes

In a skillet, crumble hamburger. Add remaining ingredients and cook stirring until hamburger is no longer pink. This can be eaten as is on a bun for a sandwich. Or add tomato sauce and cooked pasta for goulash. Or canned spaghetti sauce and cooked spaghetti for spaghetti and meat sauce. Or add tomato sauce and chili beans for chili. Save left-over unused meat for whatever you decide to have the next day.

## GRILLED TURKEY STEAK
*Maureen, daughter*

2 Pounds Pre-cooked Turkey Roast

Slice the roast into "steaks" 1/2 to 1 inch thick. Cook over hot coals for 5 minutes a side. Yield: 6-8 servings.

## CREAMED TUNA
*Helen*

2 Tablespoons Margarine
2 Tablespoons Flour
1 Cup Milk
1/4 Teaspoon Salt
Dash Pepper
1 (6 ounce) Can Water Packed Tuna, drained

Prepare a white sauce by melting the margarine in a skillet. Stir in the flour. Slowly add the milk while stirring with a wire whip. Cook over low heat until thickened. Add seasonings. Stir in drained tuna. Serve over toast. Yield: 2 servings.

## PORCUPINES
*Jessie, daughter-in-law*

1 lb. ground beef
1/2 cup uncooked rice
1/2 cup water
1/3 cup chopped onion
1 teaspoon salt
1/2 teaspoon celery salt
1/8 teaspoon garlic powder
1/8 teaspoon black pepper
1 (15 oz.) can tomato sauce
1 cup water
2 teaspoons Worcestershire sauce

Mix ground beef, rice, 1/2 cup water, onion, salt, celery salt, garlic powder and pepper. Shape mixture into small balls. Brown on all sides then drain grease from pan. Mix remaining ingredients, pour over meatballs. Heat to boiling; reduce heat. Cover and simmer 45 minutes.

*"There is not a less visually appealing dish that I can think of than creamed tuna but how we love it. Growing up, it was a staple on our table as Mom was not that crazy about fish, but she did eat tuna. Back then, we still had to eat fish all day on Fridays, so creamed tuna was served often. As an adult, it was always my fall back entrée when I had forgotten to thaw something for dinner. When Heather was young and a picky eater, I knew she would always eat creamed tuna."*

**Colleen, daughter**

**PORCUPINES**

## COCO'S CRISPY CHICKEN
*Colleen, daughter*

2 Cups All Purpose Flour
2 teaspoons Lowry's Season Salt
1 teaspoon salt
1/2 teaspoon pepper
1 Fryer, cut into pieces  (This amount of flour will coat more chicken if needed.)

Pre-heat at least 1 inch of shortening in an electric skillet to 350. Combine dry ingredients in a sack by shaking. Clean chicken. Immerse chicken in milk and drop into flour one or two pieces at a time. Shake until thoroughly covered. Place carefully into grease. Brown slightly. Turn chicken over and reduce heat to 250. Cover and cook at 250 for 30 minutes. Remove cover. Turn heat back to 350 and brown chicken. Turn it over to brown on the other side. Remove to paper towels.

## CREAM GRAVY

Strain majority of grease leaving 2 to 4 tablespoons in the pan. Add 2 to 4 tablespoons of flour to the grease in the pan, stirring constantly with a wire whip. Add 1/2 cup of milk and stir. Add heat to bring to a boil. Stir until thick. Reduce heat. Add water from potatoes while stirring with the wire whip until gravy reaches desired consistency. I season the gravy with Lowry's season salt, salt and pepper and Accent. The cracklings you strained off the grease can be added to the gravy just prior to serving.

## FRIED CATFISH
*Colleen, daughter*

1 Pound Catfish Fillets
1/2 Cup Flour
1/2 Cup Cornmeal
1/2 Teaspoon Salt
1/4 Teaspoon Pepper
1/4 teaspoon Lowry's Season Salt

Heat 1/2 to 1" grease in electric skillet to 350. Meanwhile, wash fillets. Combine flour, cornmeal and seasonings in shallow pan. Dip both sides of the fillet to coat well. Place gently in hot grease. Cook until golden. Turn and cook on other side. Drain. Serve immediately.

# Tales from the Kitchen

When Heather was a sophomore in high school, it was just the two of us at home for the first time. I worked at the high school, and at the end of her school day, she would be in my office along with her friends. Since fried chicken is one of our favorites but I didn't like to fix it for just the two of us, we invited her friends. We had to have the same accompaniments: mashed potatoes, cream gravy, cheesy peas, and Grand's biscuits. Kids who never ate peas loved the cheesy peas. Eating chicken helped strengthen her friendships, and the kids started referring to themselves as Coco's Kids and me as Momma Coco.

**Colleen, daughter**

## Pot Roast
*Helen*

2 to 2 1/2 pound boneless, chuck roast (get one that is well marbled for tenderness and flavor)
2 carrots, peeled and cut into sticks
2 potatoes, peeled and quartered (or peeled baby carrots)
1 small onion, quartered
1 teaspoon beef bouillon

Spray electric skillet with non-stick coating and pre-heat. Season roast with salt and pepper as desired. Brown in skillet on both sides. Reduce heat. Add 1 cup water, bouillon and onion. (Water measurement is an estimate. Use as much as it takes to get about 1/4-1/2 inch of water surrounding meat.) Cover and simmer for at least 2 hours. (Note: 2 hours is the minimum for it to be done. Longer cooking will lead to a more tender beef. Heather cooks hers usually 3-4 hours.) Add potatoes and carrots and continue simmering until vegetables are cooked (over 30 minutes; potatoes will take longer to cook than carrots—if making mashed potatoes for more than two people, boil additional potatoes in a separate pot). Remove meat and vegetables.

## Brown Gravy

Add a cornstarch/water mixture to the liquid in pan. Add heat to bring to a boil while stirring. Continue stirring and lower temperature, cooking until thickened. Add additional water (from potatoes) as needed. Season as desired (Lowry's, salt, pepper and Accent). Add Kitchen Bouquet. Slice beef to serve.

## Hamburger Stroganoff
*Helen*

2 Tablespoons Chopped Onion
1 pound Lean Hamburger
1/2 Teaspoon Salt
1/4 Teaspoon Pepper
1 Tablespoon Soy Sauce
1 Tablespoon Kitchen Bouquet
1 Small Can Sliced Mushrooms, drained
1 Can Cream of Mushroom Soup (10 1/2 ounces)
1/4 Cup Sour Cream
1 1/2 cups Macaroni, uncooked

Cook macaroni according to package directions. Drain. Meanwhile brown hamburger and onion in skillet. Add water and cook. Drain off water. Return hamburger to skillet. Add seasonings, mushrooms, soy sauce, Kitchen Bouquet and soup. Stir. Simmer until heated through. Just prior to serving, add sour cream. Serve over cooked macaroni. Yield: 6 servings. Preparation time: 25 minutes.

### Tips and Tricks

My mother-in-law, Harriet Rhoades, was also a good cook, and I learned several tips from her, too, including the following: Never waste the water from your boiled potatoes. Use it in the broth for chicken and noodles or pour it in the pan of gravy you're making. It helps to thicken the broth and adds flavor and vitamins.

**Nancy, daughter**

Pot Roast

**Chicken and Noodles**

"When I asked my children what recipe I should submit, the unanimous answer was chicken and noodles. Although I fix these throughout the year, they are a MUST for our family's Christmas meal. Our time together is traditionally the night before Christmas Eve, dubbed by our young sons "Christmas Adam," because "Adam" came before "Eve!" Ever since, we've called it Christmas Adam, and I always serve chicken and noodles."

**Nancy, daughter**

**Goulash**

## HOMEMADE CHICKEN AND NOODLES
*Nancy, daughter*

4-6 boneless, skinless chicken breasts. Place in large pot and cover with water seasoned with chicken bouillon, seasoned salt, pepper, and garlic. Add one onion cut in quarters, 2-3 carrots, and 2 stalks of celery. Cook 1 to 1 1/2 hours. Remove chicken and strain, saving the broth. Return the broth to the pot.

Beat 3 eggs with a couple of tablespoons of milk. Add flour and stir until just slightly sticky.. Roll out a small ball (between a golf ball and a baseball) as thin as possible on a floured cutting board.

Use a pizza cutter (if you don't have a pasta cutter) and cut 1/8 inch strips. Drop into boiling broth and stir to make sure noodles are separated. Repeat until most of the dough is used. Cut up the chicken into bite-sized pieces and add to the noodles. Cook until the noodles are tender — about 40 minutes. The flour from the noodles will thicken the broth, but you may need to add a flour paste to thicken a little more. I also add some of the water off of the boiled potatoes. (My family likes mashed potatoes with chicken and noodles.)

## OVEN BEEF STROGANOFF
*Pat, daughter*

Cut 1 to 2 lb. of steak into thin strips; chop one onion up and sauté both in a pan until not pink

Mix:
1 pkg. of stroganoff sauce
1 can of cream of mushroom soup
8 oz. pkg of cream cheese
8 oz. carton of sour cream
small jar of mushrooms
1 pkg of frozen noodles (12 oz., cooked)
1 cup (or more) of milk

Mix all ingredients; place in 9 X 13 pan; cook at 350 degrees for 45 minutes

## GOULASH
*Helen*

1 pound lean ground beef
2 Tablespoons chopped onion
1 Can Tomato Sauce
1 Tablespoon Prepared Mustard
1 Tablespoon Worcestershire Sauce
Salt and pepper to taste
1/4 teaspoon sugar
1 1/2 cups uncooked macaroni

Bring 2 quarts of water to a boil. Add macaroni and simmer for 10 minutes or until done. Meanwhile brown the hamburger in a skillet with the chopped onion. Add 1/2 cup water and continue cooking for a few minutes. Drain the hamburger using a strainer. Return the meat to the skillet. Add the remaining ingredients and simmer. When the macaroni is cooked, drain. Combine with meat mixture. Yield: 6 to 8 servings. Preparation time: 20 minutes.

## Linguine Carbonara
*Pat, daughter*

8 oz. linguine, cooked to al dente, drain
1/4 cup butter, melted
1 t. minced garlic
1/8 t. pepper flakes
1/2 t. black pepper
1/2 cup fresh mushrooms
1 cup, cooked, crumbled bacon
Sauté all in the butter for 2 minutes
1 cup heavy whipping cream

Add and bring to a boil. Add linguine and cook for 2-4 minutes. Remove from heat. Add egg, stirring quickly to prevent scrambling. Serve in hot pasta bowls with Parmesan Cheese

## Hurry Up Spaghetti Sauce
*Colleen, daughter*

1 Pound Lean Ground Beef
2 Tablespoons Chopped Onions
1 Can Hunt's Ready Italian Style Tomato Sauce (15 ounces)
1/2 Pound Spaghetti, uncooked

Prepare spaghetti according to package directions. Drain. Meanwhile brown hamburger and onion in skillet. Add water and cook. Drain water. Return hamburger to skillet. Add tomato sauce and simmer. Serve over spaghetti. Yield: 4 servings

## American Pizza
*Helen*

1 pkg yeast
1/2 cup warm water
1 egg
1/4 can tomato sauce
3 T oil or melted Crisco
1 T sugar
1 tsp salt
2 cups flour (you will need to add more as you knead)

Dissolve yeast in warm water in large bowl. Add egg and remaining ingredients, blend. Add flour and knead until smooth. Let rise until it doubles about an 1 hour. Press dough into greased sheet pan.

1 lb. of hamburger
1/2 cup of chopped onion
tomato sauce (remainder of can)
American cheese slices
1 T chili powder
salt and pepper

Brown hamburger and onion. Drain. Add seasonings. Bake at 425 for 15 minutes. Add American cheese slices to top. Bake for 5 more minutes.

**Linguini Carbonara**

*"When we hosted Mario from Costa Rica, American Pizza was his favorite and is one of my favorites from childhood."*

**Maureen, daughter**

**American Pizza**

**Hurry Up Spaghetti**

### Tuna Macaroni
*Colleen, daughter*

Small can (6 oz.) tuna, drained
1 can cream of mushroom soup (or cream of chicken or cream of celery)
3/4 cup uncooked macaroni
2 slices American cheese

Cook macaroni per directions on package. Drain. Return to pan on low heat. Add soup, tuna and cheese. Stir until cheese is melted.

### Homemade Vegetable Soup
*Helen*

Place 1-2 pounds stew meat (may also use a chuck roast or similar beef cut into cubes) into a large pot of water. Season with 2 beef bouillon cubes, seasoned salt, pepper, garlic powder, and 2 -3 tsp. sugar (optional). Boil for 4-5 hours until very tender.
Add: Chopped veggies: onion, carrots, diced tomatoes, potatoes, cabbage (a must, adds a special flavor), celery, 1 can cut green beans, frozen corn, 1 can tomato sauce, and 2-3 tbl. barley. Boil an additional 30- 45 minutes until tender.
When time is a factor, hamburger may be substituted for the stew meat. Brown, drain, and add the rest of the ingredients for a faster version of this nutritious meal.

### Broccoli Cheese Soup
*Pat, daughter*

Cook:
1/2 cup grated carrots, 1 1/2 cups water, 2 bullion cubes and 2 cups broccoli until vegetables are tender
Stir in:
1 quart 1/2 and 1/2 into which you have stirred 1/2 cup flour
Add:
1 stick butter and 1/2 lb. Velveeta
Heat on low until thick.

## Tales from the Kitchen

Tuna macaroni, or Christmas Dinner as it will forever be remembered at my household, has been a long-standing family favorite. Holiday season 2006 found me quite busy as normal. Somehow in the midst of shopping, wrapping and cooking, I forgot to plan for or purchase anything for a meal on Christmas Day. In my defense, the Henrys celebrate on Christmas Eve with a big meal. Christmas Day my girls normally go to their Dad's, so I don't worry about a big meal. That year, however, they were both here, and I hadn't planned for it. Naturally, all the stores were closed. Our good friends, the Warmowskis, when hearing of our plight, brought us a frozen pizza. I chose instead to fix a meal with what I had on hand – tuna and macaroni. Having learned my lesson, in 2007 we had a prime rib dinner!

**Colleen, daughter**

## Hurry Up Chili
*Colleen, daughter*

1 Pound Lean Ground Chuck
1 Can Brook's Chili Hot Beans
1 Can Tomato Sauce
2 Tablespoons Chili Powder
1 Teaspoon Sugar
Fresh Ground Pepper
1 Teaspoon Beef Bouillon

In large saucepan, cook ground beef thoroughly, rinsing the fat when done. Return meat to pan. Add remaining ingredients and water to achieve desired thickness. Bring to boil. Simmer a few minutes. Yield: 4 servings Preparation time: 15 minutes.

## Tips and Tricks
When chopping leafy green vegetables — like the tips of artichokes — use a scissors for ease.

**Colleen, daughter**

## Sausage Quiche
*Jessie, daughter-in-law*

1 lb. sausage, browned
2 cups shredded cheese (I use whatever I have on hand.)
6 eggs
1/2 cup milk
1 1/2 tablespoons Worcestershire sauce
1 cup hash browns with onions & peppers, thawed
1 uncooked pie shell

Mix all ingredients except pie shell. Pour into unbaked pie shell. Bake at 375 for 50-60 minutes. It is done when a knife comes out clean.

## Broccoli Rice Casserole
*Helen*

1 18 oz. pkg frozen broccoli cuts
1 cup uncooked rice, 1 beef bouillon cube
2 tbl onion and celery, butter
1 can cream of mushroom soup, 1 can milk
1 can sliced mushrooms
3-4 pieces of American cheese or Velveeta
Dash seasoned salt, pepper, garlic salt

Prepare broccoli as directed on package. Prepare rice as directed except use beef bouillon instead of salt. Cook onion and celery in butter until tender. Add soup, cheese, milk, seasonings. Combine all in 7X11 dish. Bake 350, 25-30 minutes. (May top with buttered bread crumbs before baking.)

**Broccoli Rice Casserole**

**Spinach and Artichoke Casserole**

## Spinach and Artichoke Casserole
*Jeanne, daughter-in-law (from a good friend)*

1 can (14 oz) artichoke hearts
3 10 oz. pkgs. frozen chopped spinach, defrosted
1/2 tbl. mayo
4 tbl. Butter or olive oil
6 tbl. Milk
Pepper to taste
1/3 cup fresh grated Parmesan or Romano cheese

Drain artichokes, cut up and place on bottom of a 3 quart casserole. Squeeze water from spinach and layer on top of artichokes. Blend cheese, mayo, milk, and butter. Spread on top of spinach. Sprinkle with pepper and grated cheese. Bake, uncovered, 375 degrees for 40 minutes.

## Cheesy Potatoes
*Colleen, daughter*

2 tablespoons butter
2 tablespoons flour
1/4 teaspoon salt
dash pepper
1 cup milk
6-8 slices American cheese
1 quart sliced, cooked potatoes

Peel and slice thinly potatoes. Cook in boiling water until tender about 10 minutes. Meanwhile in a skillet, melt butter over low heat. Blend in flour and seasonings. Add milk slowly while stirring with a wire whip. Cook over medium heat stirring until thickened. Reduce heat to low. Add cheese and stir until melted. Drain potatoes after cooked. Put 1/3 of potatoes in greased casserole dish. Cover with 1/3 of sauce. Cover with remaining potatoes then sauce. Stir gently to mix cheese sauce and potatoes. Note: The sauce will cook down into the potatoes so it doesn't have to be evenly distributed. Bake at 350 for 20-25 minutes or until browned. Yield: 6-8 servings.

## Broccoli Salad
*Helen (added by Laura, granddaughter)*

1 bunch of broccoli, chopped
1 cup sunflower seeds
1/2 cup raisins
1/2 lb bacon, cooked and crumbled
1/4 cup red onion
1 cup Miracle Whip
2 tablespoons rice vinegar
1/3 cup sugar

I am sure there is a correct way to mix this, but I just go in order and mix and mix and it still tastes good

— Thanks Grandma!

> "A favorite recipe is one that Grandma Henry gave me — broccoli salad. It's one of my favorites — the one I bring to potluck dinners and everyone goes oooh and ahhh over it."
>
> **Laura, granddaughter**

**Cheesy Potatoes**

## Green Beans
*Helen*

1 Pound Green Beans
2 strips Bacon
1 Tablespoon chopped Onion
1/2 Teaspoon salt
Dash Pepper
Dash Accent

Cut the bacon into 1 inch pieces and brown in sauce pan. Add remaining ingredients and water. Simmer until desired degree of doneness is achieved.

Green Beans

## Twice Baked Potatoes
*Helen*

Wash and poke desired number of potatoes. You will lose at least one-half when re-filling or when stuffing so add to number needed. Either bake in oven until done or microwave. When cooked, slice in half lengthwise. Carefully scoop out insides leaving some for shell. If you break any that's OK. They can be stuffed anyway. Prepare as for mashed potatoes (see page 8). Refill shells. Grated cheese can be added for garnish.

## Spinach with Cheese
*Colleen, daughter*

Cook entire package of spinach in microwave according to package directions. Be sure to purchase frozen, chopped spinach. Drain well using a strainer and pressing excess fluid from spinach. Add 2 slices or more of cheese and microwave an additional minute or until melted. Yield: 2-3 servings.

## Cheesy Peas
*Colleen, daughter*

2 Tablespoons Margarine
2 Tablespoons All Purpose Flour
1/2 cup milk
3 slices processed, American cheese
Dash of season salt
1/4 teaspoon salt
Dash of pepper
1 can of peas, drained

Melt margarine on top of stove in a microwaveable pan ( I use a corning ware dish.) Using a wire whip, stir in the flour then the milk. Add seasonings. Cook over low heat until thick. Add cheese and stir until melted. Remove from heat. Carefully stir in the peas. These can be prepared while the chicken is cooking then put in the microwave on high for 2-3 minutes prior to serving. ( Mom topped hers with crackers crumbs and cooked in a 350 oven for 30 minutes.)

> *"Twice Baked Potatoes are the classic potato of Henry get-togethers. We always had them with ham loaf and green beans at holidays. The only problem is now that our numbers have increased so dramatically, we don't have enough oven space to fix them."*
>
> **Colleen, daughter**

Twice Baked Potatoes

Spinach with Cheese

## CHERRY PIE FILLING SALAD
*Helen*

1 can cherry pie filling
1 can fruit cocktail, drained
2-3 bananas, sliced
1/2 cup mini marshmallows

Combine the pie filling and fruit. Chill. Just prior to serving, stir in the bananas and marshmallows. Note: This can be prepared using other fruits including fresh or frozen and any variety of fruit pie fillings. The original recipe called for apricot.

## SPARTAN CHOCOLATE CHIP COOKIES
*Nancy, daughter*

1 cup brown sugar packed
1 cup sugar
2 eggs
2 teaspoons vanilla
2/3 cup Parkay
2/3 cup butter Crisco

Cream above together until fluffy. Mix dry ingredients and stir into sugar mixture:

3 1/2 cup flour
1 tsp. baking soda
1 tsp. salt

Add 1 pkg. mini semi-sweet chocolate chips. Stir. Drop by tablespoons (I use the pampered chef small scoop) onto ungreased cookie sheet. Bake 10-11 minutes at 350 degrees. Do not overcook! Remove and cool on wire rack.

# Tales from the Kitchen

I have modified Betty Crocker's chocolate chip cookies recipe over the years. My husband coached the varsity basketball team at North Greene for 15 years, and I would make the cookies and take them to practice the night before a big game (and everyone thought Marty averaged 20 wins a year because of his coaching!) . They came to be known as "Spartan Chocolate Chip Cookies." I always thought they tasted extra good to the boys because they were so starving after practice!

**Nancy, daughter**

## GRANDMA'S SUGAR COOKIES
*Helen*

1 cup butter (do not substitute for best results)
1 cup oil
1 cup powdered sugar
1 cup sugar
2 eggs
1 tablespoon vanilla
1 teaspoon cream of tartar
1 teaspoon baking soda
1 teaspoon salt
1 quart flour

Cream both sugars, vegetable oil and softened butter. Add vanilla and eggs. Sift dry ingredients together. Stir into creamed mixture until mixed. Chill dough at this point for best results. Take a teaspoon of dough and roll into a ball. Roll in granulated sugar. Place on cookie sheet. Press down with a fork dipped in sugar. Bake at 350 for 12 minutes. Yield: 8 dozen cookies

> **Tips and Tricks**
> My aunt Maureen taught me when baking with butter, use the wrapper to grease the pan or cookie sheet before throwing it out.
>
> **Heather, granddaughter**

## PECAN SNOWBALLS
*Helen*

1/2 cup butter, softened
2-3 tablespoons sugar
1/4 teaspoon salt
1 1/2 teaspoons vanilla
1 cup ground pecans
1 cup sifted flour
1 1/2 cups powdered sugar

Cream shortening with sugar and salt. Add vanilla then flour and pecans. Form into 1" balls. Place on cookie sheet and bake at 250 for 40-45 minutes. While still hot, roll in powdered sugar. May be rolled again in powdered sugar prior to serving.

## SKILLET COOKIES
*Helen*

1/2 stick butter
1 cup sugar
2 eggs, beaten
1 (8 oz.) package dates, chopped
3 cups Rice Krispies
1/2 cup nuts
1/2 teaspoon vanilla

In saucepan, melt butter. Add sugar, eggs and dates and cook over low heat until thick. Add remaining ingredients. Form into a log. Chill. Slice and serve.

**BUTTERSCOTCH BARS**

## BUTTERSCOTCH BARS
*Helen*

2 cups brown sugar
1/2 cup Crisco
2 eggs
1 1/2 cups flour
2 teas baking powder
1 teas vanilla

Melt Crisco in pan. Turn off heat. Add brown sugar. Add the eggs and other ingredients. Pour into 9x13 pan. Bake at 350 for 20-25 minutes.

> "Lori, Kendi, and I have been known to eat the whole pan full of Butterscotch Bars."
>
> **Maureen, daughter**

## DOUBLE CHOCOLATE BROWNIES
*Jessie, daughter-in-law*

3/4 cup flour
1/4 teaspoon baking soda
1/4 teaspoon salt
1/3 cup butter
3/4 cup sugar
2 tablespoons water
1 pkg of 12 oz. semi sweet chocolate chips
1 teaspoon vanilla
2 eggs

Combine dry ingredients and set aside. In small saucepan, bring butter, sugar and water to a boil. Remove from heat. Stir in one-half the chocolate chips and the vanilla. Stir constantly until chips are melted and smooth. Add eggs one at a time beating well after each. Gradually blend in flour mixture. Stir in remaining chips. Spread into greased 9" square pan. Bake at 350 for 30-35 minutes. Note: This recipe does not double well.

**CHINESE NEW YEAR COOKIES**

> "Joe had a similar version of Chinese New Year's Cookies that he grew up with. Of course, the debate is whose is better. You decide."
>
> **Maureen, daughter**

## OAT AND CHOCOLATE BARS
*Jessie, daughter-in-law*

1 cup butter, softened
2 cups packed brown sugar
2 eggs
2 teaspoons vanilla
2 1/2 cups flour
teaspoon salt
teaspoon baking soda
3 cups uncooked quick oats

Cream together butter and brown sugar. Add eggs and vanilla. Stir in flour, salt and baking soda. Add oats; mix well. Press 2/3 of the batter into 13x9" lightly greased baking pan.

### FILLING

1 pkg semi-sweet chocolate chips
1 (14 oz.) can sweetened condensed milk
2 tablespoons butter
teaspoon vanilla
1/2 teaspoon salt

Melt chocolate chips with sweetened condensed milk, butter, vanilla and salt over medium heat, stirring constantly. Remove from heat as soon as chocolate is melted. Pour over batter in pan. Crumble remaining batter over filling. Bake 25-30 minutes or until golden brown.

**DOUBLE CHOCOLATE BROWNIES**

## SCRUMPTIOUS BROWNIES
*Jeanne, daughter-in-law*

Use 1 package of Trader Joe's Brownie Truffle baking mix and one 24.7 oz. glass jar of Trader Joe's Dark Cherries. Drain the cherries well, reserving the juice. Make the mix according to package directions. Then add 1/2 - 2/3 of cherries and stir gently. Bake according to directions. While the brownie bakes, put the juice in a small saucepan. Bring to boil and reduce heat. Simmer until the juice reduces enough to coat the back of the spoon. You can add a teaspoon of amaretto if you like. Serve the brownie with some of the reserved cherries on top and spoon sauce over.

## SNICKERDOODLES
*Colleen, daughter*

1 cup soft shortening (part butter)
1 1/2 cups sugar
2 eggs
2 3/4 cups all purpose flour
2 teaspoons cream of tartar
1 teaspoon baking soda
1/4 teaspoon salt
2 tablespoons sugar
2 teaspoons cinnamon

Heat oven to 400. Mix shortening, sugar and eggs thoroughly. Sift together dry ingredients: flour, cream of tartar, soda and salt. Stir into shortening mixture. Roll into ball the size of small walnuts. Roll in mixture of the 2 tablespoons sugar and cinnamon. Place about 2" apart on ungreased baking sheet. Bake 8-10 minutes. The cookies will puff up at first then flatten. Yield: 5 dozen cookies.

## CHINESE NEW YEAR COOKIES
*Helen*

1 cup chocolate chips
1 cup butterscotch chips
1 (5 oz.) can of chow mein noodles
1/2 cup peanuts

Melt chips over hot water or in microwave. Mix in noodles and nuts. Drop by teaspoons onto waxed paper. Chill. Yield: 4 dozen.

## CHINESE NEW YEAR COOKIES
*Joe, son-in-law*

1 cup chocolate chips
1 cup butterscotch chips
2/3 cup peanut butter
5 cups Rice Krispies

Melt chips, stir in peanut butter and Rice Krispies. Drop by spoonfuls onto wax paper.

"In grade school, parents would often bring in treats for their kids to have birthday parties at school. I would always request that my mom make Snickerdoodles because the cute boy in my class told me they were his favorite. They're so good that I used to sell them to a neighbor in Manhattan by the dozen."

**Heather, granddaughter**

SNICKERDOODLES

CHOCOLATE CHIP COOKIES

## CHOCOLATE CHIP COOKIES
*Maureen, daughter*

1 stick butter
1/2 cup Crisco
3/4 cup sugar
3/4 cup brown sugar
2 eggs
1 tsp vanilla
1 tsp baking soda
1 tsp salt
2 3/4 cup flour
1 cup chocolate chips

Beat butter and Crisco. Add sugars, blend well. Add eggs one at a time. Add vanilla. Mix baking soda, salt and flour and add. Stir just until mixed. Add chocolate chips. Spoon onto greased cookie sheets. Bake at 350 for 9 minutes. (We like ours gooey not crispy. You can adjust time)

# Tales from the Kitchen

When we were growing up, we would often go swimming at Aunt Nancy's house. Mom would sometimes bring a dessert, and with the heat of the summer, Congo Sqaures were a favorite for their short baking time.

When I got older, Maureen was raving about the caramel icing that goes on them. "What icing?" Beth and I asked.

Apparently, we did not warrant the full treat as Mom never made it. Needless to say now that we know there is an icing, we don't skip it like our mom. They are such a family favorite, that Beth even requested them as her 28th birthday "cake."

**Heather, granddaughter**

A favorite for bake sales, Mom would always cut and plate the cookies and leave only the outside edge of the Congo Squares for us kids!

Although Colleen's girls never knew the delicious pleasure (because she would take a shortcut and skip the icing), the icing is what sets these bars apart.

**Maureen, daughter**

## Congo Squares
*Helen*

2/3 cup shortening
2 1/4 cups brown sugar
3 eggs
2 3/4 cups flour
2 1/2 teaspoons baking powder
1/2 teaspoon salt
1 cup chopped nuts
1 (6 oz.) package chocolate chips
1 teaspoon vanilla

Melt shortening and add brown sugar. Stir until well mixed; cool. Add eggs one at a time beating well after each. Sift together dry ingredients. Add to cooled mixture along with the nuts, chips and vanilla. Pour into greased jelly roll pan. Bake for 25 minutes at 350. Ice with frosting, if desired.

### Frosting:
1 cup brown sugar
5 tablespoons evaporated milk
1 tablespoon butter
1 1/2 cups powdered sugar
1 teaspoon vanilla

In a small saucepan, cook together the brown sugar, evaporated milk and butter. Bring to a boil. Cool. Add powdered sugar and vanilla. Spread on cooled cookies.

## Strawberry Pizza
*Jessie, daughter-in-law*

1 tube refrigerated sugar cookie dough
4 oz. cream cheese, softened
1 cup powdered sugar
1 1/2 cups cool whip
1 carton strawberry glaze
1# fresh strawberries, cleaned and sliced

Press sugar cookie dough onto a pizza pan to make one big cookie. Bake until lightly brown. Cool. Mix cream cheese, powdered sugar and cool whip until smooth. Spread over cookie.
Then spread the strawberry glaze over the cream cheese mixture.
Then spread sliced strawberries over the glaze. Refrigerate.

> **Tips and Tricks**
> Always break your eggs into a separate cup before adding to other ingredients.
>
> **Maureen, daughter**

Congo Squares

CREAM PUFFS

"At holidays, we usually have so many desserts that they cover the entire dining room table. It is not unusual to have more desserts than main course dishes. In the Henry family, we have a bit of a sweet tooth. In fact, I once had my sisters over to dinner, and we made five different desserts. When Nancy opened the fridge to get the Cool Whip, she accused me of holding out on her for not offering a blackberry pie that I made for my daughter, Beth, who just gave birth. Nancy pointed out that they had all had kids, too."

**Colleen, daughter**

## CREAM PUFFS
*Helen*

1/2 cup water
1/4 cup butter
Heat to rolling boil.

1/2 cup flour
Stir in. Keep stirring over low heat until mixture forms a ball.

2 eggs
Beat into cooked mixture all at once until smooth.

Drop by scant 1/4 cupfuls about 3 inches apart onto ungreased cookie sheet. Cook at 400 degrees until puffed and golden. Cool. Cut off tops and fill with cream filling. Top with fudge sauce or fudge icing.

## FILLING FOR CREAM PUFFS

1 3/4 cups milk
1/4 cup white Karo Syrup
Scald

1/4 cup milk
4 T. cornstarch
Mix

1/2 cup sugar
pinch salt
Add to cornstarch mixture. Beat 3 egg yolks. Add to cornstarch mixture. Add mixture to scalded milk. Cook and stir until thick. Cover and cook 5 more minutes. Cool and add 1 t. vanilla.

## RUM BALLS
*Helen*

2 1/2 cups finely crushed vanilla wafers
1 cup powdered sugar
1 cup chopped nuts
2 tablespoons cocoa
3 tablespoons corn syrup
1/4 cup light rum or 1 teaspoon rum extract and 3 tablespoons cream

Combine crumbs, sugar, nuts and cocoa. Stir in remaining ingredients and mix well. Shape into 1" balls. Roll in additional powdered sugar or shake in bag. Let season in an airtight container in a cool place for 2-3 days, if possible.

## Pumpkin Cupcakes
*Jessie, daughter-in-law*

2 cups sugar
1 small can pumpkin
1 cup oil
4 eggs
2 cups flour
1/2 teaspoon salt
2 teaspoons cinnamon
2 teaspoons baking soda
1 tablespoon baking powder

Combine sugar, pumpkin, oil and eggs. Stir in remaining ingredients and mix well. Pour into cupcake pans, mini cupcake pans or 15 x 10" baking pan. Bake at 350 until done. Baking time will vary depending upon whether you made a cake, cupcakes or mini cupcakes.

### Frosting:
8 oz. cream cheese softened
1 stick margarine or butter, softened
1 quart powdered sugar
1 teaspoon vanilla

Combine all ingredients and beat until fluffy. Ice cupcakes when cool. Refrigerate after icing.

## Oatmeal Cake
*Nancy, daughter*

1 1/4 cup boiling water
1 cup oats
1/2 cup softened butter
1 cup sugar
1 cup brown sugar
1 tsp. vanilla
2 eggs
1 1/2 cup flour
1 tsp. soda
1/2 tsp. salt
3/4 tsp cinnamon
1/4 tsp nutmeg

Pour water over oats, stir and let stand several minutes. Cream butter. Add sugars. Blend in vanilla and eggs. Stir into prepared oats. Add dry ingredients and blend. Pour into greased 9-inch square pan or 8X11. Bake 350 degrees for 35 to 40 minutes.

### Frosting:
3/4 stick melted butter
3/4 cup brown sugar
4 tbl. cream
1/2 cup chopped pecans
1 cup coconut

For frosting, combine all ingredients and spread over finished hot cake. Broil until bubbly (only about 1 minute).

**Pumpkin Cupcakes**

*"Birthday parties always involved elaborate cakes following delicious potlucks with the cousins."*

**Nancy, daughter**

**Oatmeal Cake**

## Mississippi Mud Cake
*Jessie, daughter-in-law*

2 sticks butter or margarine
4 eggs
2 cups sugar
teaspoon vanilla
2 tablespoons cocoa
1 1/2 cups flour
1 (7 oz.) jar marshmallow cream

Cream butter, sugar, eggs and vanilla. Add flour and cocoa. Bake at 350 in floured 13x9" baking pan for 25-30 minutes. Do not overbake. Cool and then spread with marshmallow cream. Then top with fudge icing.

### Fudge Icing:
1 stick butter
1 quart powdered sugar
teaspoon vanilla
1/2 cup evaporated milk
1/2 cup cocoa

Mix until smooth and spread over marshmallow cream.

## Fruit Cocktail Cake
*Helen*

2 cups flour
1 1/2 teaspoons soda
1/8 teaspoon salt
1 1/2 cups sugar

## Tales from the Kitchen

For Dan's 24th birthday, Jessie made his favorite Mississippi Mud Cake, along with a spread of party hats, jelly beans, balloons, and milk in crystal wine glasses.

**Dan, son**

2 eggs, beaten
#303 can fruit cocktail, undrained

Sift flour, soda and salt together into a large mixing bowl. Add remaining ingredients and stir to combine. Pour into 8x8" pan that has been sprayed with non-stick spray. Cook at 350 for 40 minutes. Note: Can be sprinkled with mixture of brown sugar, cinnamon and nuts prior to baking.

## Strawberry Cake
*Helen*

1 pkg. white cake mix
1 pkg (3 oz.) strawberry gelatin
2 tablespoons flour
4 eggs
1/2 cup water
1/2 box (10 oz.) frozen strawberries
3/4 cup oil

Beat together the cake mix, gelatin, flour, eggs and water for 2 minutes. Add strawberries and beat an additional 1 minute. Add oil and beat another minute. Bake at 350 in 9 x 13" pan for 35-40 minutes. Cool. Ice with strawberry frosting.

## Icing

1/2 cup butter or margarine, softened
1# confectioners' sugar
1/2 box (10 oz.) frozen strawberries
1/2 teaspoon vanilla

Beat butter until smooth. Add sugar alternately with strawberries. Beat until smooth. Add vanilla. If it is too thick, milk can be added. If too thin, add more confectioners' sugar.

## Pumpkin Pie Cake
*Helen*

4 eggs, slightly beaten
1 can (16 oz) pumpkin (2 cups)
1 1/2 cups sugar
1 tablespoon pumpkin pie spice
1 teaspoon salt
1 can (13 oz) evaporated milk
1 box yellow cake mix
1 cup melted butter
1 cup chopped pecans

Combine eggs, pumpkin, sugar, spices and salt. Stir in milk. Pour into ungreased 9 x 13" pan. Sprinkle dry cake mix over filling. Pour melted butter over top. Sprinkle with pecans. Bake at 350 for 1 hour, or until set. Serve with whipped cream.

**Tips and Tricks**
A quality knife is worth the extra cost.

**Maureen, daughter**

JIFFY FRUIT COBBLER

"*Agner's advice to our children: Take family road trips. Each year the six of us — and sometimes extras — would pile in the van and explore the country. The benefits: extended family time; lessons in patience and tolerance; expanded views on geography, history, people and food. Our trips often involved camping. One of the kids' favorite fireside desserts was a cobbler Joe made in a cast iron Dutch oven nestled in the fire. You can make it without the fire or mosquitos. (See Colleen's microwave version.)*"

**Maureen, daughter**

## GERMAN CHOCOLATE CAKE
*Helen*

1 pkg Bakers German Sweet Chocolate
1/2 cup boiling water
2 1/2 cups sifted cake flour
1 t. soda
1/2 t. salt
1 cup butter
2 cups sugar
4 eggs, divided
1 t. vanilla
1 cup buttermilk

Melt chocolate, water. Sift dry ingredients. Cream together butter and sugar. Add egg yolks to butter mixture. Add vanilla and buttermilk to butter mixture and then add chocolate and lastly flour mixture. Beat egg whites until stiff peaks form. Fold into mixture. Pour into 3 9" pans. Bake at 350 for 35 to 40 minutes.

### FROSTING:
1 cup evaporated milk
1 cup sugar
3 egg yolks
1/2 cup butter
1 t. vanilla

Cook and stir until thick
Cool, then add 1 1/3 cups coconut
and 1 cup pecan pieces. Stir. Let cool. Then ice tops of the three layers of cake.

## JIFFY FRUIT COBBLER
*Joe, son-in-law*

2 cans cherry, peach, apple, or blueberry pie filling (We sometimes do 1/2 and 1/2)
2 small boxes yellow Jiffy cake mix, dry
1 stick butter, melted

Put pie filling in 9x13 pan. Joe likes to warm this in the oven. Sprinkle on cake mix. Drizzle melted butter. Bake at 350 for 20-30 minutes until golden. Serve with ice cream.

## CHERRY DUMP CAKE
*Colleen*

1 (20 to 22 ounce) can cherry pie filling (or any flavor can be used)
1 box Jiffy yellow cake mix
1/4 cup cold margarine, thinly sliced

Spread pie filling in 8 inch round microwave dish. Microwave on high for 4 minutes, stirring after 2 minutes until heated through. Sprinkle the dry cake mix over the fruit. Distribute the margarine slices over the cake mix. Microwave at high for 11 to 13 minutes rotating the dish 1/4 turn after 6 minutes if you do not have a carousel. Serve warm with ice cream. Yield: 6 servings. Total preparation time: 20 minutes.

## Graham Streusel Cake
*Pat, daughter*

3/4 cup butter
2 cups graham crackers, crushed
3/4 cups nuts
3/4 cups brown sugar
1 t. cinnamon

Mix all above (this is streusel mix)

1 cup water
3 eggs
1/4 cup oil
1 pkg. butter pecan or yellow cake mix

Mix above (this is batter). Pour 1/2 batter into greased/floured cake or Bundt pan. Top with 1/2 streusel mix. Cover with rest of batter. Top with remaining crumbs. Bake at 350 for 45 minutes.

## Glaze
When cool, glaze with 1 cup of powdered sugar mixed with 2 t. water

## Hot Fudge Sauce
*Helen*

1 can evaporated milk
1 stick (1/2 cup) butter or margarine
4 unsweetened chocolate squares (4 ounces)
3 cups sugar
1 teaspoon vanilla
dash salt

Melt chocolate squares and butter over low heat in heavy saucepan. Slowly stir in the sugar. Add the evaporated milk to sugar solution slowly. Cook over low heat until it barely boils. Add vanilla and salt. Serve over ice cream or the following ice cream desserts.

## Brownie Baked Alaska
*Helen*

1 Chocolate Cake Mix
6 Eggs, separated
Water
1/2 gallon vanilla ice cream
Sugar
1 teaspoon vanilla
Cream of tartar

Combine cake mix, egg yolks, and water. Stir until smooth. Spread in 9 x 12" baking pan. Bake at 350 for  minutes. When cool, freeze. Soften ice cream and spread on frozen chocolate cake. Freeze. Whip egg whites and cream of tartar until stiff. Add sugar and continue beating until firm peaks form. Beat in the vanilla. Pre-heat oven to 350. Spread egg whites on ice cream. Swirl to make peaks. Bake for  minutes or until egg whites brown slightly. Watch carefully as you don't want to over-bake. Freeze until serving. Drizzle with hot fudge sauce. This is an elegant dessert that can be prepared days ahead of its use.

---

*"When I was first getting to know my 'cousin' Steve (our grandmothers are sisters), we were talking about food and both started raving about our grandmothers' hot fudge recipe. We started comparing notes and realized it was the same recipe (though we both claimed ownership for our grandmother). That's when I realized what family is about; out there in the world, someone I didn't even know was being raised with the same values, traditions ... and hot fudge as me. Family, and food, involve sharing what is important."*

**Heather, granddaughter**

Brownie Baked Alaska and Hot Fudge Sauce

# HOMEMADE ICE CREAM
*Colleen, daughter*

1 Quart milk
2 cups sugar
1/3 cup flour
2 eggs

Cook 1 quart milk and 1 cup of sugar in microwave at high for 3 minutes, stir, 3 minutes, stir, then 2 minutes. (It should be close to scalded depending on the power of your microwave.) Meanwhile combine the eggs, 1 cup sugar, and the flour to make a paste. Using a wire whip, slowly stir into the hot milk solution. Microwave at high for 2 minutes, stir, 2 minutes, stir, 2 minutes, stir until thick. Cool in refrigerator. Stir several times while cooling. Place cooked solution in ice cream freezer container. Stir in:
1 quart half and half
1 quart milk
1 teaspoon vanilla
Crank until frozen to desired thickness. Be sure to add salt to your ice to facilitate the freezing process.

## Tales from the Kitchen
Nikki rolls a pie crust early in her baking career. She learned well from her mother. We have always loved this picture of Nikki holding her cherry pie that she baked earlier. You can just see how proud she is of it, and how young she started learning to bake.

**Dan, son**

## Mint Stuff
*Nancy, daughter*

2 cups crushed Oreos (This can be done in a blender a few at a time.)
4 Tablespoons butter or margarine
Mix crushed Oreos and melted butter and press into a 9 x 12 baking pan. Freeze.

1/2 gallon mint chocolate chip ice cream, softened
Spread ice cream on cookie crust. Freeze.

4 Tablespoons butter or margarine
2 squares unsweetened chocolate (2 ounces)
1 1/2 cups sifted powder sugar
2-3 Tablespoons milk
1 teaspoon vanilla
Melt butter and chocolate squares. Add powdered sugar, milk and vanilla. Beat until smooth. This will be runny. After this cools, spread quickly on the ice cream. Freeze until serving. Yield: 12 servings

## Aunt Kate's Lime Sherbet
*Kate, sister*

1  3 ounce Package Lime Jello
3/4 cup sugar
1/2 cup boiling water
Juice from one lemon
juice from one orange
2 Cups milk
Combine Jello and sugar. Pour water over and return to boil. Cool.
Stir in the juices and milk. Freeze in shallow pan for hours. Remove from freezer. Beat. Freeze until solid.

## Stir in the Pan Pie Crust
*Jessie, daughter-in-law*

1 1/2 cups all purpose flour
1 1/2 teaspoons powdered sugar
3/4 teaspoon salt
1/2 cup oil
2 tablespoons milk

Combine the flour, sugar and salt in the pie pan. Stir together the oil and milk. Using a fork, stir the oil/milk combination into the flour mixture. Press along bottom and up sides of the pie plate. Crimp. Bake at 450 for 8-10 minutes.

PECAN PIE

> "The one lesson that has really stuck with me was when I made a meringue on a butterscotch pie and did not seal the meringue. When I removed the pie from the overn, I had a little glob of meringue in the center. I have never forgotten that lesson and never made that mistake since."
>
> **Colleen, daughter**

STRAWBERRY PIE

## BASIC PIE CRUST (FOR ONE)
*Helen*

1 cup all purpose flour
1/3 cup plus 1 tablespoon lard
1/2 teaspoon salt
2-3 tablespoons water

Combine the flour and salt. Cut the lard in until it resembles small peas. Lightly stir in the water until just combined. Roll out on wax paper sprinkled with flour. Gently fold the crust in half and then half again. Place in pie plate and unfold. Gently press down and up sides to eliminate any trapped air. For one crust pie, crimp top. Using a fork, prick bottom and sides. Bake at 450 for 10-12 minutes.

## PECAN PIE
*Helen*

1 cup white karo syrup
1 cup sugar
1 teaspoon vanilla
3 eggs, slightly beaten
1/8 teaspoon salt
2 tablespoons melted margarine
1 cup pecans
unbaked pie crust

Combine the syrup, eggs, sugar, salt and vanilla in a large bowl. Stir in the pecans. Pour into 9" unbaked pie crust. Bake at 400 for 15 minutes. Reduce heat to 350 and bake for an additional 30-35 minutes.

## STRAWBERRY PIE
*Helen*

3 tablespoons strawberry gelatin powder
3 tablespoons cornstarch
1 cup sugar
1 cup water
1 quart strawberries, stemmed and halved
1 Keebler Shortbread crust

In microwave safe bowl, combine gelatin, cornstarch and sugar. Whisk in water. Microwave at high for 2 minutes, stir, microwave 2 minutes, stir. Repeat until mixture thickens. Time will vary depending upon power of microwave. Refrigerate until cools down but not too thick. (If the solution is too hot, it will draw out the moisture from the strawberries and will by runny.) Pour over strawberries. Pour into shell. Refrigerate until set. Note: This can be made successful with sugar free ingredients. Also any baked pie crust will work for this. Also it can be made this with other fresh berries and with fresh peaches substituting the appropriately flavored gelatin.

## Peanut Butter Fudge Pie
*Pat, daughter*

1/4 Cup Corn Syrup
2 Tablespoons Brown Sugar
3 Tablespoons Butter
2 1/2 Cups Rice Krispies

Cook corn syrup, brown sugar and butter until it boils. Pour over cereal. Stir gently. Press into 10" buttered pie plate.

1/2 Cup Creamy Peanut Butter
1/2 Cup Fudge Sauce
1/3 Cup Corn Syrup

Heat until smooth. Spread on cooled crust. Freeze until firm (2-3 hours).

1/2 Gallon Vanilla Ice Cream, softened
Scoop into frozen crust. Freeze 4 hours or overnight.
1/2 Cup Chopped Peanuts
1 Cup Fudge Sauce
Sprinkle 1/4 cup nuts over ice cream. Top with fudge sauce, then end with remaining nuts. Freeze until served. Yield: 8 servings.

## Caramel Pecan Pie
*Helen*

42 Kraft caramels (Brock's are not a good substitute)
1/2 cup water
6 T butter
3 eggs
1 1/8 cup sugar
3/8 teas salt
3/4 teas vanilla

Heat caramels, water and butter until melted. Combine remaining ingredients in a bowl and add to caramel mixture. Stir in 1 cup pecan halves. Pour into prepared, uncooked pie crust. (If you are using small crusts this recipe will fill two crusts). Bake at 400 for 15 minutes then lower temperature to 350 for 25 minutes longer. You really have to watch closely, it is challenging to get this baked to the perfect consistency.

## Peanut Butter Bon Bons
*Colleen, daughter*

1 1/2 Pounds Peanut Butter
1 1/2 Sticks Butter or Margarine, softened
1 Pound Powdered Sugar
3 Cups Rice Krispies
16 ounces Hershey's Milk Chocolate Bars
1/2 Bar Paraffin

Using an extra large mixing bowl, cream together the peanut butter and margarine until smooth. Slowly add the powdered sugar and mix until it becomes too stiff to add any more powdered sugar. Then work remainder in with your hands. Add rice krispies and work with hands. Chill. Form into small balls (teaspoon size) and place on waxed paper on a cookie sheet. Chill for at least 30 minutes. Meanwhile in double boiler, melt the milk chocolate and paraffin. Keeping the chocolate hot, dip the balls into the chocolate. Remove with fork and place on waxed paper. Chill. (We usually freeze them to help them set up and to preserve them longer.)

**Peanut Butter Bon Bons**

*"When my daughters used to help me make peanut butter bon bons as little girls, they would roll them into worms because they were easier than balls. Each year they still make a worm."*

**Colleen, daughter**

**Peanut Butter Fudge Pie**

**Carmel Pecan Pie**

## Individual Cheesecakes
*Maureen, daughter*

1 box vanilla wafers
3 (8 oz.) packages cream cheese, softened
1 1/2 cups sugar
1 1/2 tablespoons lemon juice
1 1/2 teaspoons vanilla
3 eggs
1 large can cherry pie filling

Mix cream cheese, sugar, lemon juice and vanilla. Add eggs one at a time beating well after each. Place one wafer in the bottom of a cupcake liner lined muffin tin. Fill 2/3 full with cheesecake mix. Bake 15 minutes at 375. Cool. Top with cherries. Refrigerate or freeze.

## Microwave Caramel Corn
*Jessie, daughter-in-law*

1 cup brown sugar
1 stick margarine
1/4 cup white corn syrup
1/2 teaspoon salt
1/2 teaspoon baking soda
3-4 quarts popped corn

Combine all ingredients except soda and popcorn in 1 1/2 to 2 quart dish. Bring to a boil in microwave then cook 2 minutes. Remove from microwave and stir in soda. Put popped corn in brown grocery bag. Pour syrup over corn. Close bag and shake. Cook in bag in microwave for 1 1/2 minutes. Shake and cook another 1 1/2 minutes. Pour into pan and allow to cool.

# Tales from the Kitchen

Jeff cooks oysters for Thanksgiving dinner and cooks with his brother, Greg, when they were younger. Jeff and his sisters, Kathy and Kristina, and brother, Greg, all like to cook. I thought it was important that even the boys learn to cook when they were growing up, so now both Greg and Jeff cook a lot for their families.

**Pat, daughter**

## CARAMEL PECAN CINNAMON ROLLS
*Jessie, daughter-in-law*

Dough:
1 pkg yeast
1/2 cup warm water
1/2 cup lukewarm milk (scalded then cooled)
1/3 cup sugar
1/3 cup butter
1 teaspoon salt
1 egg
3 1/2 - 4 cups flour
1/2 cup butter, softened
1/2 cup sugar
4 teaspoons cinnamon
Topping:
2 cups butter, melted
1 cup brown sugar
1/4 cup corn syrup
1 cup pecans

Dissolve yeast in warm water. Stir in milk, sugar, 1/3 cup butter, salt, egg and 2 cups flour. Beat until smooth. Mix in enough remaining flour to make dough easy to handle. Knead dough about 5 minutes. Place in greased bowl. Cover and let rise until double. Punch down dough. Roll dough into large rectangle. Spread with softened butter. Mix sugar and cinnamon and sprinkle over butter. Roll up tightly beginning on long side of rectangle. Cut into 1 1/2" slices. Combine topping ingredients in bottom of 13 x 9" pan. Place rolls in pan over topping. Let rise until double. Bake at 375 for 30 minutes or until very brown. Invert pan on cookie sheet.

## Ham loaf

Ham loaf is the traditional Henry family Christmas Eve dinner — a little scary to the kids but the adults love it that way because it leaves more for them. Scott made this T-shirt (a spoof of "Wedding Crashers") as an homage to one of his favorite Grandma Helen recipes.

## ENGLISH TOFFEE
*Maureen, daughter*

1/2 Pound Butter
1 Cup Sugar
2 Tablespoons Water
1 Tablespoon White Karo Syrup
4 to 5 Hershey's Milk Chocolate Bars
Chopped Pecans, if desired

Combine the butter and sugar in saucepan and bring to full boil on stove. Add the water and Karo. Cook to 300 degrees (hard crack). Don't go over this as it will burn. Spread in buttered jelly roll pan. Top immediately with Hershey bars and let melt. Spread chocolate if needed. Top with chopped pecans, if desired. Cool. Break into chunks. This freezes nicely.

INDIVIDUAL CHEESECAKES

# New Additions
Third generation contributions

### SPINACH ARTICHOKE DIP
*Nikki, granddaughter*

1 teaspoon garlic powder
1 (10 oz.) pkg. frozen spinach, thawed and drained
1 (14 oz.) can artichoke hearts, drained and chopped
1 Alfredo pasta sauce (I use garlic Parmesan.)
1 cup shredded mozzarella
1/3 cup grated Parmesan
4 oz. cream cheese, softened

Mix together all ingredients and bake covered in a pie plate for 30 minutes.

# Hot Crab Dip
*Heather, granddaughter*

1 (8 oz) container of soft cream cheese
1 1/2 cups milk
1 cup mayonnaise
1 T prepared horseradish
2 (6 oz.) cans of crab meat, drained (I like to use two different kids for variety — like one lump and one pink, for example.)
1/8 tsp. celery salt
1 cup white cheddar cheese, shredded

Combine the cream cheese, milk, mayonnaise, horseradish, crab meat, and celery salt. Mix until creamy. Spread mixture into an 8x12 inch baking dish and bake for 35 to 40 minutes. Remove the mixture from the oven. Cover the top with cheddar cheese. Bake until the cheese is melted. Meanwhile, cut pita bread into triangles. Baste with butter and bake until toasted (5-10 minutes). Serve together.

# Taco Dip
*Brian, grandson*

Layer the following in platter or large bowl:
1 can refried beans
1 small carton sour cream
1 small bottle of taco sauce
1 head of lettuce (use as much lettuce as you like)
1 bag shredded cheese
1 tomato (dice up and sprinkle on top)

Eat with nacho chips.

# Kathy's Dip
*Kathy, granddaughter*

2 C sharp cheddar cheese, shredded
6 green onions, chopped
12 pieces bacon, crumbled
3/4 C silvered almonds, toasted
1 C Hellmann's Mayonnaise

Mix together all and chill. Serve with crackers.

# Bacon Horseradish Dip
*Brett, grandson*

8 oz. cream cheese, softened
10-15 slices crispy bacon, chopped
3 tablespoons horseradish

Mix all ingredients and serve with chips.

**Tony's Chipped Beef Dip**

"Our dad made the Chipped Beef Dip from a recipe he got from Henry VanTuyle, a member of mom and dad's bridge club. When he was in high school, our son Tony fixed it quite often and it came to be known as 'Tony's Dip.'"

**Nancy, daughter**

**Buffalo Chicken Dip**

## Nacho Dip
*The Tobin siblings, grandchildren*

1 8 oz. cream cheese, softened
1 jar of taco sauce
2 cups Mexican or sharp cheddar cheese
sliced black olives
2 cups shredded lettuce
1/2 cup black beans, drained and rinsed
1 tomato, chopped
4 green onions, sliced
1 lb. taco meat (optional)
Package of chips for dipping

Spread the cream cheese on a serving platter. Top with 1/2 of the taco sauce. Sprinkle on the lettuce, cheese, onions, olives, tomatoes and black beans. If you like, top with taco meat and sour cream. Drizzle taco sauce over all. Serve with dipping chips

## Buffalo Chicken Dip
*Beth, granddaughter*

8 oz. cream cheese
16 oz. sour cream
1 C. blue cheese dressing
1/2 C. buffalo style hot sauce
8 oz. provolone cheese - grated
2 1/2 C. cooked chicken
celery, carrots, crackers

Preheat oven to 350. Soften cream cheese, beat together with sour cream and dressing until smooth. Add buffalo sauce and beat until smooth. Stir in grated cheese and chicken. I like to buy an already cooked rotisserie chicken from the store and use it. (It will take just over half the chicken). Spread in 9 X 13 cake pan. Cook for 30 to 40 min. until bubbling on the edges. Makes 6 1/2 cups. As it makes so much, I have frozen half of the recipe and saved for later. You can defrost in the refrigerator overnight and bake a similar amount of time.

## Tony's Chipped Beef Dip
*Tony, grandson*

Cream 1 pkg softened cream cheese with 1 heaping tbl. Miracle Whip (may need to add a little more Miracle Whip). Add seasonings (dash garlic salt, garlic powder, seasoned salt, pepper), 1 tablespoon of horseradish and 2 tsp. chopped onion, dried or fresh. Cup up small pkg. of Buhlig's beef and stir in. Serve with potato chips or crackers.
We usually triple the recipe, using 1 large pkg. of the beef.

## BRUSCHETTA
*Beth, granddaughter*

1 fresh tomato
1 ball of fresh mozzarella (look in the fancy cheese portion of the supermarket-it is a soft, white cheese)
3-4 leaves of fresh basil
1 mini loaf of French bread
olive oil
garlic salt

Dice tomato into 1/2 inch by 1/2 inch squares. Snip basil into small pieces. Stir tomato and basil with 2 Tbs. olive oil, add dash of garlic salt. Set mixture aside in refrigerator. Slice mozzarella into 1/4 inch slices, and halve. If you have an egg slicer, this works amazingly well to slice the mozzarella because it is soft, and getting a narrow slice can be difficult with a knife. Slice bread into 3/4 inch slices and halve vertically. Brush olive oil on bread slices and toast until golden brown. A toaster oven works well for this, but can be done in the regular oven (just makes your house hotter). I like to arrange the bread on one side of a pretty plate with the mozzarella on the other and a bowl of the tomatoes in the middle. Serve with bread on bottom, then mozzarella, and tomato mixture on top.

## SAN ANTONIO SALSA
*Carolyn, granddaughter-in-law*

Combine in a food processor or finely chop:
1/2 bunch cilantro
1/2 sweet onion
3-4 tomatoes
1-2 jalapenos
2 cloves garlic
2 limes squeezed

Sprinkle cumin, salt, and pepper to taste. Serve with chips. Bueno!!!

## BLACK BEAN AND CORN SALSA
*Nikki, granddaughter*

1 can black beans, rinsed
1 can shoepeg corn, drained
1 can diced tomatoes with chilies
1/2 jar chunky salsa
1 teaspoon ground cumin
1 tablespoon lime juice
salt to taste

Mix all ingredients together. Serve with nacho chips.

*"To me, bruschetta is the essence of summer. Fresh tomatoes and basil, cool mozzarella. Served with a chilled Pinot Grigio, it is all you need for a summer night on the deck. This is easy to make, and it makes a lovely addition to any summer night."*

**Beth, granddaughter**

**BRUSCHETTA**

*"When Steve was in the Air Force stationed in Texas, San Antonio Salsa was a favorite for us."*

**Carolyn, granddaughter-in-law**

## FLATBREAD
*Brett, grandson*

1 pkg. yeast
1 cup hot water (not boiling)
1 tablespoon sugar
3/4 teaspoon salt
1/4 cup oil
3 cups flour

Mix yeast, water and sugar and let stand 5 minutes. Add the salt, oil and 2 1/2 cups flour. Mix well. Knead in the last 1/2 cup flour. Let rise 30 minutes. Pre-heat non-stick skillet to med/high heat. Take a fist sized ball of dough and roll into a circle to fit skillet. Put into dry skillet and cook until browned. Turn over and brown the other side. We use this bread with hamburgers, chicken salad or anything you would normally use a bun for.

## MONKEY BREAD
*Amanda, granddaughter-in-law*

4 tubes premade biscuit dough
2 t. cinnamon
1/2 cup sugar
1 cup brown sugar
1/2 cup Parkay or butter

Preheat oven to 325. Cut each biscuit into 4 pieces. Put cinnamon and sugar together in a plastic bag. Place biscuit pieces into the bag and shake until well coated. Put coated pieces into buttered bunt pan. Melt butter and add brown sugar. Pour brown sugar/butter mixture over the top of the coated pieces. Bake for 35-40 minutes.

## Tales from the Kitchen

Our kids (Kaylie, Hannah, Braylon and soon Eli) all love to "help" me around the house, especially in the kitchen. A recipe they particularly love to make is Monkey Bread, which is not only fun to make but is also easy and delicious. They are so proud to tell Daddy (Tony) that they made it all by themselves just for him, although they end up eating most of it themselves!

**Amanda, granddaughter-in-law**

## Banana Bread
*Lori, granddaughter*

1 1/4 cups sugar
1/2 cup butter (1 stick)
2 eggs
1 tsp. baking soda
1 tbl. Vanilla
1/4 cup yogurt
2 to 3 brown bananas
1 1/2 cup flour
1 tsp. salt

Cream sugar and butter. Add the eggs. Mix the baking soda into the yogurt. Add the yogurt to the mix. Add bananas that have been mashed lightly. Add vanilla and salt. Slowly add the flour. Lightly grease baking pan. Pour mixture in. Bake 50-60 minutes at 350 F.

## Sherried Beef
*Michael A., grandson*

3 lb stew meat
2 cans cream of mushroom soup
1/2 pkg Lipton Onion soup mix-dry
2/3 C cooking sherry
1 small can mushrooms

Mix all ingredients in a dutch oven (oven proof pan) cook at 325 for 3 hours stirring occasionally. Serve over cooked noodles.

## Italian Chicken
*Heidi, granddaughter-in-law*

4 Boneless Skinless Chicken Breasts
1 16 oz jar of sliced pepperoncinis
1 packet of Italian Dressing mix
Water
Hoagie rolls

In slow cooker, combine all the ingredients and cook on high for about 2 or 3 hours. Then turn in to low. The longer it cooks the more flavor it gets. Tear up the chicken into pieces and you can make a sandwich. Pat likes to eat it on hoagie rolls with swiss cheese. I like provolone. It doesn't have to be eaten as a sandwich. It can also be eaten as chicken breasts.

## Beany Burgers
*Nikki, granddaughter*

1 lb, ground beef, browned and drained
1 can pork & beans
1/2 cup catsup
1/4 cup BBQ sauce
3/4 teaspoon chili powder
salt and pepper to taste

Mix all ingredients and heat through. Serve on buns.

*"My Lola (grandma) used to marinate chicken this way all the time, but you can also use this on pork, beef, and seafood too. I loved it when she grilled wings using this marinade. I think I'm five, all over again."*

**Edwina,
granddaughter-in-law**

ITALIAN CHICKEN

*"In our house, we are all about quick, easy meals during the week. This crock pot recipe for Italian chicken is just that, and it makes a delicious meal!"*

**Jen R.
granddaughter-in-law**

### LOLA'S MARINADE
*Edwina, granddaughter-in-law*

1 cup Vegetable Oil
1 cup Soy Sauce (Kikoman)
1/2 cup Lemon Juice, freshly squeezed
1 teaspoon Black Pepper, ground
1/2 teaspoon Sugar
2 cloves Fresh Garlic, smashed

### ELENI'S GREEK MARINADE
*Edwina, granddaughter-in-law*

1 cup Extra Virgin Olive Oil
1/2 cup Lemon Juice, freshly squeezed
5 cloves Fresh Garlic, chopped
1 teaspoon Dried Oregano, crushed
1/2 teaspoon Black Pepper, ground

### ITALIAN CHICKEN
*Jen R., granddaughter-in-law*

4 chicken breasts (frozen)
1 package of dry Italian dressing
Half a jar of mild banana peppers and juice
1/2 C. of water

Put all ingredients in a crock pot and let them cook on low for about 5 hours. Take a utensil and shred the chicken. Add a roll and you have a great main course for very little work!

### STICKY CHINESE CHICKEN
*Nikki, granddaughter*

1/2 cup crouton (crushed)
2 teaspoons garlic powder
1 lb skinless chicken breast (cut into 1 inch cubes)
1 tablespoon soy sauce
1/8 cup cornstarch
1/8 cup canola oil

In large bowl, whisk crouton crumbs, garlic powder, and cornstarch. Stir in the soy sauce. Add chicken and toss until completely coated. Cover, refrigerate for at least 30 minutes. Heat the oil in a large nonstick skillet over medium heat. Add chicken and cook, covered for 20-25 minutes until nice and crispy and cooked through. Turn about 4/5 times during cooking to avoid burning. Drain on paper towels. Serve over rice with optional soy sauce.

### SOUR CREAM CHICKEN
*Brett, grandson*

4-6 boneless chicken breasts
1 can cream of mushroom soup
16 oz carton sour cream
1 pkg. dry Ranch Dressing mix

Put chicken in shallow baking pan. Mix the remaining ingredients. Spread on chicken. Bake at 375 for 1 hour or until chicken in done. Do not turn chicken during baking.

## Chicken & Chilis
*Michael A., grandson*

4 boneless skinless chicken breasts cooked & shredded (or use a roaster chicken)
1 can cream chicken soup
1 can chopped tomatoes and chilis
3 cups cojack cheese
1 pkg Nacho Cheese Doritos

Mix chicken soup with tomatoes & chilis. Layer ingredients in a casserole beginning with a layer of Doritos, 1/2 the chicken, 1/2 the soup mixture, 1/2 the cheese. Repeat layering. Heat in microwave until heated through and cheese is melted.

**Chicken & Chilis**

## Tim's Tasty Tuna
*Tim, grandson*

1 can of tuna.
As much mayo as desired.
Crackers or bread (for a sandwich)

Mix mayo and tuna in the bowl. Then put on crackers or bread. (Or feed your cat — ha ha)

*"As a busy family, Chicken Pie is something that is easy to make and all four of my kids love it."*
**Megan, granddaughter-in-law**

## Chicken Pie
*Megan, granddaughter-in-law*

whole chicken or 3 chicken breasts
1 can cream of chicken soup
1-2 cans of biscuits

Boil whole chicken for 1 hour or 3 chicken breasts for 45 minutes. Let cool, and then shred. Keep broth for later. Put shredded chicken in botton of 9x13 pan. Mix 1 can of cream of chicken soup and 1 cup of the broth together in bowl. Pour over the chicken. Place biscuits on top of chicken and mixture. I sometimes tear biscuits into two pieces depending on the size. Bake using the directions for the biscuits. Let set for a while to thicken up.

**Chicken Pie**

## Hamburger Corn Pie
*Nikki, granddaughter*

1 lb. ground beef
1/4 lb. pork sausage
1 small onion, chopped
1 clove garlic, chopped
1 can diced tomatoes
1 can corn, drained
1 small can sliced black olives, drained
2 1/2 teaspoons chili powder
1 1/2 teaspoons salt
1 cup shredded Cheddar cheese
1 pkg. corn bread mix

*"I do seriously eat Tim's Tasty Tuna!"*
**Tim, grandson**

Brown ground beef and sausage with onion and garlic. Drain. Stir in tomatoes with liquid, corn, olives, chili powder and salt. Heat to boiling. Pour into ungreased 13 x9" baking dish. Fix cornbread mix per directions on package. Pour over mixture. Sprinkle with cheese. Bake at 350 for 40 minutes or until golden brown.

**Hamburger Corn Pie**

## Long Boy Cheeseburgers
*Mike and Angie, grandson and granddaughter-in-law*

1 lb ground beef
1 tsp salt
1/2 tsp black pepper
1 Tbs Worcestershire Sauce
1/4 cup finely chopped onion
1/2 cup Cornflake crumbs
1/2 cup evaporated milk

Mix all ingredients in a large bowl. Cut one loaf of french bread lengthwise. Spread mixture on bread. Place on a baking sheet. Bake for 25-45 min at 350 degrees until cooked (depending on thickness of the meat). Place slices of American Cheese on the top and melt. Cut into 3" pieces. (Trim loaves shorter if needed to fit in oven.) Serves: all kids and Mike

## Chicken Enchilada Quiche
*Nikki, granddaughter*

1 refrigerated pie crust
4 eggs, whisked
1 cup milk
1 1/2 cups canned chicken, drained
1 1/2 cups broken tortilla chips
2 cups shredded Monterey Jack cheese
1 cup shredded sharp Cheddar cheese
1 cup chunky salsa
1 small can chopped green chiles
1/2 teaspoon salt

Place pie crust in deep dish pie pan. Mix together remaining ingredients. Pour into pie crust. Bake at 350 for 55-65 minutes. Let stand 10 minutes before serving.

# Tales from the Kitchen

When it came to food back when I was a kid, I was pretty simple. Whenever I wanted a snack I would go into the kitchen and grab a loaf of bread and start eating on it. That's right, just plain bread. And maybe a glass of milk... anyway, I digress. We had a space heater that we would sometimes use during the winter and one day while "snacking," young and naive enough to not know how toast really works, I thought to myself, "I wonder how the bread would taste when it's warmed up." So I went over to the space heater, took a piece of bread and held it up close for an ample amount of time, took a bite and IT WAS TOAST! HOW COOL! Needless to say, after my incredible discovery, I ate most of my bread as toast whenever the heater was on. When she cleaned, Mom would always be so confused as to how crumbs were getting into the space heater.

**Brettt, grandson**

## ENCHILADA ROLLS
*Scott, grandson*

2 cups coarsely chopped cooked chicken
1/4 cup chopped pitted ripe olives
1 (4 ounce) cup shredded Mexican blend cheese
1 (4 ounce) can chopped green chilies, undrained
1/2 cup mayonnaise
1 tablespoon Cajun seasoning (or any general seasoning)
1 plum tomato
1 tsp lime juice
2/3 cup finely crushed corn tortilla chips, divided
2 (8 ounce) packages refrigerated crescent rolls
1 cup salsa
1 cup sour cream

Preheat oven to 375 F. Place chopped chicken and olives in mixing bowl. Add cheese, green chilies, mayonnaise, and seasoning mix. Chop 1 tomato. Add chopped tomato and lime juice to chicken mixture. Reserve 2 tablespoons crushed chips; add remaining chips to chicken mixture and mix well. Sprinkle reserved crushed chips over cutting board. Unroll crescent dough. Place dough, sticky-side down, onto crushed chips; press down lightly, so chips adhere to dough. Separate dough into triangles. Arrange triangles, chip side down, in a circle on round baking stone (or round pizza baking sheet) with wide ends overlapping in the center and points towards outside. Scoop chicken mixture evenly onto the wide ends of each triangle. Bring points of triangles up over filling and tuck under wide ends of dough at center of ring. (Filling will not be completely covered.) Bake 20-25 minutes or until golden. Cut and serve with salsa and sour cream.

## ADOBO
*Edwina, granddaughter-in-law*

3 + 3 tbs. vegetable oil
2 pounds chicken with bone and skin on
3-4 pounds pork shoulder, cut into 1.5" cubes
1 fist fresh garlic, peeled and crushed
20 pieces whole peppercorns
2-3 pieces dried bay leaves
1/2 cup cider vinegar (not white)
1 cup soy sauce (Kikoman)

> "My mother always told my little brother that the girl he marries must be able to make a great adobo. If she puts onion in it, she's failed."
>
> **Edwina, granddaughter-in-law**

Heat the oil in a large dutch oven-type pot, and brown the chicken and pork in 3 batches, and set aside. Add the remaining 3 tablespoons of oil to the empty pot, and cook the garlic until it is light gold in color. Return the meat to the pot, add enough water to cover half the meat, and bring to a boil. Reduce the heat to medium-high, and stir in the peppercorns, soy sauce, and bay leaves. Place the stir spoon in the opposite end of the kitchen. Add the vinegar and cover the pot with the lid. Do not stir after adding the vinegar. After you have let the vinegar cook for 15 minutes, stir the mixture, and continue cooking for an additional 15 minutes. Taste, and if needed, add 1 more tablespoon of soy sauce for a saltier taste, and one tablespoon vinegar for a more sour taste. If you do add more vinegar, remember not to stir until you have allowed it to cook off another 5 minutes. Let stand for 10 minutes before serving. Serve with plain white rice and ripe banana slices (not plantain) if desired. This dish tastes even better if eaten the next day and the next if there's any left.

LONG BOY CHEESEBURGERS

> "Clam Chowder is one of Jeff's favorite recipes. He cooks it in large quantities at the KC Club for New Year's Day each year."
>
> **Pat, daughter**

Clam Chowder

> "Three years I won first place at the Bank of America chilli cookoff with my chilli recipe!"
>
> **Scott, grandson**

Scott's Grand Guinness Chili

## CLAM CHOWDER
*Jeff, grandson*

(for about 2 quarts)
2/3 cup (4 oz.) diced salt pork
1 T. butter
3 cups sliced onions
1 bay leaf
3/4 cup crumbled "common" crackers
4 cups liquid: clam juices and water or fish stock or light chicken broth
1 pound sliced or diced potatoes (3 to 3 1/2 cups)
salt and ground white pepper
2 cups milk or light cream
24 ounces of canned clams (juice included), diced or minced

Blanch the salt pork by simmering in saucepan with 1 quart of water for 5 minutes. Sauté slowly with the butter in the saucepan until it begins to brown (about 5 minutes). Stir in the onions, add bay leaf, cover, and cook slowly 8 to 10 minutes until onions are tender and translucent. Blend in crackers. Pour 4 cups of liquid into the onion pan. Add the potatoes. Bring to a boil and simmer for 20 minutes. Blend in the milk/cream. Bring to the simmer. Taste and season. Add clams. Warm and serve.

## SCOTT'S GRAND GUINNESS CHILI....BRILLIANT!
*Scott, grandson*

1 cup onions (diced)
1 cup green peppers (diced)
3 garlic cloves (minced)
2 lbs. ground beef
1/4 cup jalapeno peppers (diced)
1 tsp Tabasco
1 tsp onion powder
1 tsp garlic salt
1 tsp cumin
1/2 tsp black pepper
2 tsp salt
1 T Cajun seasoning or other seasoning salt
1/2 tsp crushed red pepper
1/4 cup chili powder
1 cup Guinness
1-2 bay leaves, crushed
1 (16 oz) chopped chili tomatoes
1 (16 oz) can tomato sauce
1 tsp Worcestershire sauce
2 T honey
1 (16 oz) can kidney/chili beans

Heat a few tablespoons of veg. oil in a large skillet. Stir-fry the onions, green peppers, and garlic for 5-10 min. until tender. Add ground beef to skillet and cook until brown. Drain meat mixture. In a crock-pot or kettle, mix all remaining ingredients together. Add meat mixture to crock pot and stir well. Simmer on low heat for 3-4 hours. Enjoy!

## Chicken Chili
*Beth, granddaughter*

1 Pound Skinless, Boneless Chicken Breast, cut into cubes
1 Jar Salsa
1 Can Diced Tomatoes for Chili
1 Can Tomato Sauce
1 Can Cooked Navy or Pinto Beans

Brown chicken in large saucepan. Cook over low heat until done (10 to 15 minutes.) Add remaining ingredients. Heat thoroughly. To serve: dip it with nacho chips. Yield: 4 to 6 servings. Note: regular stewed tomatoes can be used if you don't want such a spicy soup. We've used any combination of tomatoes, sauce and salsa and still get a good product.

**Chicken Chilli**

## Chili Supreme
*Brittany, granddaughter-in-law*

2 bags Chiliman chili mix
2 lbs. hamburger, browned
1 lb. sausage, browned
2 16 oz cans red beans, drained
1 16 oz can stewed tomatoes
1 8 oz can mushrooms, drained
1 6 oz can tomato sauce
1 1/4 C. Ketchup
1 C. water
1 med. onion, chopped
4 stalks celery, chopped
1 T. brown sugar
1 T. peanut butter

Cook 6 to 8 hours in a crockpot.

"One of Greg's favorite things to do- is barbeque for a group. This photo happens to be at his son, Ben's house after an Illinois College football game."

**Pat, daughter**

## Taco Soup
*Cathy, granddaughter-in-law*

2 pounds ground beef
1 large chopped onion
1 pkg. taco seasoning
2 cans tomato soup
2 cans chopped tomatoes
2 cans stewed tomatoes
2 cans corn with juice
2 cans red kidney beans, drained
1 can sliced black olives
1 jar salsa
1 can water

Brown ground beef with onion in large pot. Drain fat. Add remaining ingredients and bring to a boil. Simmer. When serving, top with your choice of chopped green opinions, chopped red, green or yellow peppers, shredded cheddar cheese, crushed taco chips or sour cream.

**Taco Soup**

## TOMATO-BASIL SOUP
*Kristina, granddaughter*

4 cups tomatoes (8 to 10) peeled, cored and chopped, or 4 cups canned whole tomatoes, crushed
4 cups unsalted tomato juice
12 to 14 fresh basil leaves, plus additional for garnish, chopped
1 cup whipping cream
1/2 cup sweet, unsalted butter, softened
1/4 t. cracked black pepper
Salt to taste
Crusty bread

Combine tomatoes and juice in saucepan. Simmer for 30 minutes over medium-low heat. Cool slightly, then place in a blender or food processor. Add basil and process to puree; this will have to be done in batches. Return mixture to saucepan. Add cream and butter. Stir over low heat until butter and cream are incorporated. Stir in salt and pepper before serving. Garnish with more fresh basil and serve with fresh, crusty bread. Makes 8 servings.

## BROCCOLI CHEESE SOUP
*Brittany, granddaughter-in-law*

1 pkg. frozen, chopped broccoli
1 can cream of onion soup
1 can cream of celery soup
1 stick butter
1 sm. jar of Cheez Whiz
1 qt. half & half

Prepare broccoli, drain. Put the rest of the ingredients in a large pot, heat on high until boiling, stirring vigorously to avoid sticking. Then add the broccoli and heat a few minutes more.

## Tales from the Kitchen

Growing up, I chose ham and peas tortellini for my birthday dinner every year. It was a dish that I made for Brian at the beginning stages of our relationship (to win him over). Tortellini became our "signature" dish that we always make together (usually while listening to Frank Sinatra and drinking wine), always striving to perfect it. This year we made it for our one year anniversary, complete with fresh basil from our new garden in our first home together

**Lori, granddaughter**

## JAMBALAYA
*Mark, grandson*

1 teaspoon vegetable oil
1/2 lbs Cubed Ham
1/2 lbs Smoked Hot Sausage (John Morrell), chopped
3/4 cup Onion, chopped
3/4 cup Green Bell Pepper, chopped
3/4 cup Tomatoes, seeded and chopped
1 can Campbell's Cream of Chicken Soup with herbs
1.5 cans water (use soup can)
1 package Lipton/Knorr Spanish Rice
1 tablespoon Worcester Sauce
1 teaspoon Black Pepper
1/2 teaspoon Red Pepper
1 teaspoon Garlic, minced (fresh or dried)
1/2 teaspoon Dried Basil
1/2 teaspoon Thyme

Preheat the oven to 350 degrees. Prepare a 9x13 glass Pyrex pan by greasing it or spraying it with nonstick cooking spray. Heat oil in skillet on low heat. Add the ham, sausage, onion, green bell pepper, and tomatoes. Sauté until the onion is soft. Increase the heat to medium. Stir in the soup, water, rice, and Worcester sauce. Add the spices (black and red pepper, garlic, basil, and thyme). Continue to stirring occasionally for 10 more minutes. You want some of the water to evaporate, but not all of it. Pour entire mixture into prepared pan. Cover with foil and bake for 40 minutes. Remove the foil and bake for another 10 to 15 minutes. (Add shrimp at your own risk!)

## HAM AND PEA TORTELLINI
*Lori, granddaughter*

Boil 18 oz. of cheese tortellini (2 small packages)

In a sauce pan combine:
1 pint of 1/2 and 1/2 (We use fat free.)
1 Tb butter
salt, pepper to taste
2 large garlic cloves
8 fresh basil leaves
1 tsp. to 1 Tb. corn starch
Let that simmer for a bit in the pan

Add to sauce:
3 slices of prosciutto
1 cup frozen peas (Defrost in microwave first and then add to sauce.)
3 Tb to 1/4 cup (enough to cover the top of the pan) grated Parmesan. Add during last few minutes.
Serves four (Although we usually eat almost all of it!)

GRANDMA'S LASAGNA

*"My lasagna recipe actually comes from the other side of my family, but it was something my grandmother never shared with me before she passed away. My mother and I, using our memories and cooking knowledge, recreated the recipe after her death. Despite how simple it is, it became one of my signature meals as a young cook in college. I even shared it with a friend as a wedding gift, and he still tells me about how he enjoys when his wife makes it."*

**Heather, granddaughter**

## TOMATO AND ZUCCHINI PASTA
*Lori, granddaughter*

In a large saute pan over medium heat
2 Tb. butter
1 garlic clove, finely minced
1/2 large zucchini
2 pinches of sea salt
pepper to taste
15 to 20 cherry tomatoes
4 to 5 chive stems, diced
1/4 cup Parmesan, grated
Whole wheat linguine pasta (enough for 2 servings)

In a sauce pan, heat all ingredients besides pasta. Boil pasta according to directions. Rinse and drain pasta. Add noodles to sauce pan. Toss noodles with sauce and add a tsp. of e.v.o.o.

## BLAKE'S FAVORITE PASTA BAKE
*Blake, grandson-in-law*

1 box round noodles (rigatoni, penne, mostaccoli)
2 T. olive oil
2-3 cloves garlic, chopped
4 ripe medium tomatoes, chopped
1/2 T. oregano
1/2 T. basil
Salt and pepper to taste
1 - 8 oz. bag of mozzarella
4 oz. grated Parmesan
Garlic powder (optional)

Preheat oven to 400 degrees. Cook pasta according to package, drain. Heat oil in pan, add garlic and cook for about a minute, careful not to burn it. Add tomatoes and cook until tender, add spices. Let the mixture cook for a couple minutes. Grease or spray a deep casserole dish. Put half of the drained, cooked pasta in the dish, pour half of tomato mixture onto pasta, sprinkle half of the cheeses on top. Add another layer of pasta, tomato mixture, cheeses. If you'd like an extra garlic flavor, sprinkle some garlic powder over the top. Bake uncovered about 10-15 minutes or until the cheese is a golden brown.

## GRANDMA'S LASAGNA
*Heather, granddaughter*

9 lasagna noodles, cooked
3 cans of Hunt's tomato sauce
1 1/2 lb. of hamburger
1 6 oz. container of small curd cottage cheese
18 oz. of shredded Mozzarella cheese
Parmesan cheese
garlic powder

Cook lasagna noodles according to package instructions. Meanwhile brown hamburger. Drain grease from hamburger and add tomato sauce, leaving a bit of sauce to line the bottom of your casserole pan. Add garlic powder to taste. Place three noodles on top of sauce in pan. Spoon 1/3 of cottage cheese on top of noodles. Cover with 1/3 of sauce. Shake Parmesan cheese over sauce, and cover with Mozzarella. Repeat steps for next two layers. Cover with aluminum foil and bake at 350 for 45 minutes to 1 hour.

## SPINACH LASAGNE
*Carolyn, granddaughter-in-law*

9 lasagna noodles
1 bag 16 oz. shredded mozzarella cheese
Mix in a bowl:
16 oz Ricotta cheese
1 bag fresh baby spinach (sliced or diced)
2 cloves garlic

## SPAGHETTI SAUCE
(You can substitute 26 oz jar of your favorite sauce)
Combine and heat on stove top:
6 tomatoes diced
2 cloves garlic
basil and oregano to taste
1 can tomato sauce
1 can tomato paste (if needed)

Boil lasagna noodles (No bake noodles will also work.) Use 9x13 and begin layers: Sauce, noodles, 1/3 spinach mixture. Sauce, mozzarella, noodles, 1/3 spinach mixture. Sauce, mozzarella, noodles, 1/3 spinach mixture, sauce, mozzarella. Bake 350 for 1 hour.

## PANCIT
*Edwina, granddaughter-in-law*

2 tablespoons vegetable oil
3 cloves fresh garlic, chopped
1/2 yellow onion, sliced
1/2 pound raw chicken breast, cut into 1/2" cubes
5 pieces shiitake mushrooms (hydrate in hot water if in dried form), sliced
1 cup carrots, julienned
1 cup celery, sliced thin
2 cups cabbage, sliced thin
2 packages chow mein noodles or any egg noodle (not La Choy)
1/2 cup oyster sauce
1/2 cup soy sauce
1 cup chicken broth
1 teaspoon ground black pepper

Prepare the noodles according to the directions on the package. If it is dry, you will need to soak the noodles in hot/boiling water for 2 minutes before draining. If it is frozen, you will need to blanch the noodles in hot/boiling water for 2 minutes before draining. Similarly, if the shiitake mushrooms are dried, you will need to soak it in hot water for 10-15 minutes to hydrate. Heat the oil in a super-large skillet or wok. Add the garlic and onions, stirring occasionally until the garlic is light gold. Add the chicken and mushrooms, and stir until the chicken is almost cooked through. Add the carrots, celery, oyster sauce, pepper, and chicken broth. When the carrots are almost soft, add the cabbage and cook for another minute. Stir in the noodles and cook for another 5 minutes, or until the noodles soak up all of the broth. Season with the soy sauce, and let stand for 5 minutes before serving. Serve with lemon or lime wedges.
**Option:** You may use the Filipino rice stick noodle (bihon) for a lighter version. Rinse the noodles and drain. Do not soak them. Increase the chicken broth to 2 cans. Add the noodles to the broth when it begins to boil. Omit the oyster sauce, and replace it with equal amounts of soy sauce, for a total of 1 cup.

*"My brother makes this lasagna for our family when he visits."*
**Carolyn, granddaughter-in-law**

**TOMATO AND ZUCHINI PASTA**

*"My grandmother always made sure we had pancit on our birthdays. The noodles, when cooked, are not only long, but also expand when hydrated, symbolic of a long and healthy life. The colorful vegetables in this dish represent a colorful life full of adventure and contentment."*
**Edwina, granddaughter-in-law**

## PAD THAI
*Scott, grandson*

1 (8 oz) package rice noodles
3 tablespoon fish sauce (caution – this stuff stinks!)
2 tablespoon sugar
1 1/2 tablespoon tomato paste
1 tablespoon water
1 tablespoon Worcestershire sauce
2 teaspoon lime juice
2 teaspoon chili-garlic sauce, aka Sambal Oelek
2 eggs
2 tablespoon vegetable (or other) oil
4 cloves of garlic
1 tsp crushed red pepper
1 lb. of your choice of protein (chicken, shrimp, pork, or tofu) cut into 1" cubes
2 tablespoons crushed peanuts
1 cup bean sprouts
1 cup chopped green onions
1/2 cup cilantro (optional)

Boil noodles as instructed on noodle packet — typically boil for 5-10 minutes until tender, then drain and rinse with cold water. Drain and set aside. Mix in a bowl the fish sauce, sugar, tomato paste, water, Worcestershire, lime juice and Chili-garlic sauce. Set aside. Scramble 2 eggs and cook until done. Set aside. Heat oil in large wok or frying pan. Add garlic, crushed red pepper, and choice of protein. Stir-fry until meat is cooked. Add sauce mixture, crushed peanuts, and scrambled eggs, then stir-fry for 2-3 minutes. Add drained rice noodles and stir-fry until evenly coated. Stir in bean sprouts, green onion, and cilantro. Continue to stir-fry for 2-3 minutes.

## Tales from the Kitchen

When I was about 7 years old I had already tried baking things on my own, but always with my mom's supervision. When she would go to work and my older brother was babysitting me, she always cautioned me not to use the mixer by myself. I wanted to bake a cake one day, and decided to take her at her word. I gathered together all of the ingredients and followed the recipe, except the part about blending it all with an electric mixer. I mixed all of it by hand. It was difficult and took a while, but I was happy with it. I started the oven (on my own, without adult supervision) and baked it. I baked it the right amount of time, but the cake turned out flat — more like brownies. I think that was my lesson learned for trying it on my own!

**Nikki, granddaughter**

## Meat Sauce for Spaghetti
*Cathy, granddaughter-in-law*

2 T. olive oil
1 green or red pepper
1 medium onion, diced
1 lb. ground beef
1 can (29 oz.) tomatoes
2 cans (8 oz.) tomato sauce
1 can (3-4 oz) sliced mushrooms
2 t. salt
1/8 t. Cayenne pepper
2 T. chopped parsley
1 bay leaf
1/2 t. oregano
1 cup dry red wine

Heat oil in saucepan. Add green (or red) pepper and onion and cook until tender. Add beef and brown. Stir in remaining ingredients. Cover and simmer for 1 to 1/2 hours. Serve over your favorite pasta.

## Pasta Salad
*Carole, granddaughter-in-law*

12 oz. rontina pasta, cooked
Fresh, chopped broccoli
Chopped red and/or green pepper
Black olives
3/4 cup Parmesan cheese
1/2 red onion, chopped
Mix with 12 oz. of zesty Italian dressing.

## Merrigan's Chicken Salad
*Kristina, granddaughter*

4 boneless, skinless chicken breasts, cooked in white wine
1 stalk celery, chopped
chopped onion, to taste
1 cup Hellman's mayonnaise
splash of red wine vinegar
1/4 t. Lawry's seasoning salt
freshly ground pepper
dill to taste

Cut chicken into biter size pieces. Mix with celery and onion. In a separate bowl combine mayonnaise, vinegar and seasonings. Combine dressing with chicken. Chill.

Pasta Salad

BROCCOLI RICE CASSEROLE

## SPINACH/KRAUT SALAD
*Mike and Angie, grandson and granddaughter-in-law*

1 12 oz. bag of spinach
1 20 oz. can of sauerkraut
1/3 cup of salad oil
1 tsp salt
2-3 Tbs of sugar
1/4 cup of cider vinegar

Drain Kraut. Mix with spinach. Pour dressing on salad just before serving. Toss. Serves: 6

## CROCK POT BEANS
*Brett, grandson*

1 lb. cubed ham
2 1/2 cups mixed dried beans
2 cups diced tomatoes
1 large onion, chopped
2 carrots, chopped
1 tablespoon Italian seasonings
1 teaspoon salt
1 teaspoon black pepper
1/4 teaspoon ground red pepper
1 large can tomato juice

Mix all ingredients and cook in crock pot for 8 hours.

> "Greg's typical position is in the kitchen the morning following any holiday. He loves to make breakfast for everyone and his speciality is biuscuits and sausage gravy. This is very hearty and rich with sausage. Greg usually triples the recipe as everyone loves his biscuits and gravy."
>
> **Pat, daughter**

## BROCCOLI RICE CASSEROLE
*Carole, daughter-in-law*

1 small jar Cheez Whiz (8 oz.)
1 can cream of mushroom (or celery) soup
3/4 stick of butter
1 1/3 cup Minute Rice (uncooked)
1/2 cup chopped celery
1/2 cup of chopped onion
1 pkg. (10 oz) of thawed, chopped broccoli (or same amount of fresh)

Mix Cheez Whiz and soup together. Add all other ingredients. Pour into a creased casserole dish. Cook at 350 degrees for 35 to 40 minutes

## HEARTY BISCUITS AND SAUSAGE GRAVY
*Greg, grandson*

1 pound any good sausage such as Bob Evans
Milk or 1/2 and 1/2
Bullion cubes
Salt and pepper to taste

Brown the sausage, then add flour or Bisquick to the sausage/fat in the pan. Add two cups of milk and stir until desired thickness, adding milk or Bisquick if needed. Add one pork or beef bullion cube for each cup of milk. Add a little salt and pepper to taste. Serve over Bisquick biscuits or refrigerated biscuits

HEARTY BISCUITS AND SAUSAGE GRAVY

# Blueberry-Sour Cream Breakfast Cake
*Edwina, granddaughter-in-law*

## Filling
1/2 cup brown sugar, packed
1 teaspoon cinnamon
1/2 cup pecans or walnuts, chopped

## Dry Ingredients
2 cups cake flour (you can use regular flour and sift it)
1/4 teaspoon salt
1 teaspoon baking powder

## Wet Ingredients
1 cup butter
2 cups sugar
2 large eggs
1 cup sour cream
1 teaspoon vanilla

## Celebrity Ingredient
1 cup Fresh Blueberries (or thaw some frozen ones)

Prepare a bundt pan by greasing it and dusting it with flour. Preheat the oven to 350 degrees. Prepare the filling by mixing the brown sugar, cinnamon and nuts together. Set aside. Sift together the dry ingredients and set aside. Cream the butter and sugar until light and fluffy; add eggs. Fold in sour cream and vanilla. Add the dry ingredients and mix for 2 minutes (with electric mixer). Fold in blueberries. Pour 1/3 batter into the bundt pan and sprinkle half of the filling over it. Pour the next 1/3 batter over the top and sprinkle with the remaining filling. Top with remaining batter. Gently swirl cake with a knife or spatula. Bake for one hour or until the toothpick test comes out clean. Cool and invert onto a serving platter. Dust with powdered sugar.

# Mickey Pancakes
*Kendi, granddaughter*

1 1/4 flour
3 tsp. baking powder
1 T. sugar
1 tsp. brown sugar
1/2 tsp. salt
1 egg white, beaten
1 cup milk
1 tsp. vanilla
1 T. butter, melted

\* Add a half mashed banana, a half cup of blueberries, or a handful of walnuts or chocolate chips to the batter for an extra treat

Mix all dry ingredients in a mixing bowl, set aside. Mix all liquid ingredients together and add to the dry ingredients. Add the 'extra treats' if you'd like. Butter a hot griddle and pour desired amount of batter onto griddle (2 small circles for the ears, 1 larger circle for the face). Flip pancakes when you see bubbles. Serve with a smile!

---

*"One of our favorite family meals is brunch. Kathy Langdon cooked caramel pecan rolls, cinnamon muffins and egg casseroles. She is shown with her two sons, Patrick and Joe."*

**Pat, daughter**

**Mickey Pancakes**

*"Can you think of any morning better than one that includes brown sugar, cinnamon, and nuts swirled with blueberries? Everyone raves about this one, even if they don't get to lick the batter bowl clean. I think the batter is the best part – it tastes like rich vanilla ice cream."*

**Edwina, granddaughter-in-law**

## Breakfast Casserole
*Jen R., granddaughter-in-law*

7 slices of bread
1 C. cheddar cheese
1 lb sausage (Italian has more flavor)
1 C. Mozzarella cheese
6 eggs
1 tsp. Worchester sauce
1 C. cream or half and half
salt and pepper to taste
mushrooms (optional)

Brown sausage and let cool. Lay bread on the bottom of a 9x13 greased baking dish. Layer sausage and cheese on top. Mix all other ingredients together and pour over the bread, sausage, and cheese. Bake for 45 minutes at 350 degrees. (I usually prepare everything and let it sit overnight. Then in the morning I bake it.)

## Candied Pecans
*Nikki, granddaughter*

1 cup packed brown sugar
2 cups pecan halves
1 tablespoon vanilla
1 teaspoon cinnamon

Combine all ingredients in small bowl. Stir well to coat pecans. Bake in 13 x 9" greased pan for 12 minutes at 350, stirring once. Pour out on greased baking sheet and separate nuts. Store in air tight container.

## Tales from the Kitchen

Breakfast casserole has been a tradition in my family on holiday mornings for many, many years. This past Christmas, Matt, Kamille, and I had our first Christmas morning at our house. Of course, I made breakfast casserole. Eager to continue the tradition that I have done for quite a while, we all sat down at the table to eat. Kamille took one bite, scrunched up her face, and let the casserole dribble out of her mouth. She followed that by saying, "uck." Matt looked at her and laughed, then looked at me and said, "I agree Kam, I have never liked this stuff." That Christmas morning, we tossed the casserole and had cereal. Here's to new traditions!

Despite the fact that I will never be making this for my family Christmas morning, I love this dish! I usually take it to work for special days and it is a crowd favorite. I hope you will enjoy it too!

**Jen R., granddaughter-in-law**

## Fluffy White Chocolate Chip Meringue Bars
*Kendi, granddaughter*

1 box Chocolate Fudge cake mix
1/2 cup butter softened
4 T milk
1 box Fluffy White Frosting Mix (Betty Crocker)
1/2 C pecans
1/2 C chocolate chips

Combine dry cake mix, butter and milk. Press into ungreased 9 x 13 pan. Bake crust at 350 for 10 minutes. While this is baking, mix frosting mix as directed with 1/2 C boiling water. Remove crust and spread frosting over. Sprinkle on pecans and chips. Return to oven for 10-15 minutes longer.

## Oreo Dessert
*Cathy, granddaughter-in-law*

12 oz Cool Whip
8 oz cream cheese
1 cup powdered sugar
Cream the above.

2 3 oz. pkg. instant vanilla pudding mix
4 cups of milk
Make according to directions and combine with Cool Whip mixture.

20 oz. pkg. of Oreos, crushed Layer two times with Oreos ending on top. Top with gummy worms.

*"All the Langdons are cookie lovers so they never last overnight."*

**Pat, daughter**

Oreo Dessert

*"Rolo Pretzel is an easy peanut-free, egg-free yummy treat. Hannah's favorite!"*
**Carolyn, granddaughter-in-law**

**Chilled Pineapple Banana Dessert**

*"Steve's favorite dessert is Chilled Pinapple Banana Dessert. This was one of the first dessert's Steve had with my family and when we were dating during our college years, my mom would make this for him when he visited. He still asks for it to this day."*
**Carolyn, granddaughter-in-law**

## Rolo Pretzel
*Carolyn, granddaughter-in-law*

Buy 1 package of Tiny twists pretzels (15 oz)
2 packages Rolo's candy

Preheat oven to 325. Place pretzels on cookie sheet or jelly roll sheet. Put 1 Rolo on each pretzel. You will be able to fill 2 sheets. Bake for 3-5 minutes till the Rolo's start to melt. Remove from oven and gently place a pretzel on top. (Rolo is sandwiched between 2 pretzels.) Refrigerate and serve.
**At Christmas time we put Hershey peppermint kisses on top instead of the pretzel**

## Peanut Butter Sauce
*Nikki, granddaughter*

1 cup sugar
1 tablespoon white corn syrup
1/4 teaspoon salt
3/4 cup milk
6 tablespoons peanut butter
1/2 teaspoon vanilla extract

Mix sugar, corn syrup, salt and milk. Cook over low heat, stirring constantly until thickened. Add peanut butter; mix well. Remove from heat and let cool. Add vanilla. Serve peanut butter sauce over a warm brownie and vanilla ice cream.

## Chilled Pineapple Banana Dessert
*Carolyn, granddaughter-in-law*

2 cups graham cracker crumbs
1 stick melted butter
Combine and press into bottom of 9x13 glass dish. Save some crumbs to sprinkle on top.

2 cups powdered sugar
4 Tablespoons butter or margarine, softened (1/2 stick)
3 oz cream cheese ,softened
1/4 cup milk
1 tsp vanilla

Cream butter and cream cheese. Add milk and vanilla. Slowly beat in powdered sugar. Beat until creamy and fluffy. Slice 4-5 medium bananas length-wise and place over desert. Drain can of crushed pineapple and place over bananas. Spread 1 container of cool whip over pineapple and sprinkle remainder of graham cracker crumbs over the cool whip. Refrigerate for 2 hours. Enjoy!!!!!

## Gooey Butter Cake
*Carole, granddaughter-in-law*

1 pkg. yellow cake mix
1 stick butter
2 eggs
Mix and spread in 9X13 pan (will be stiff).

1 lb. powdered sugar
2 eggs
8 oz. cream cheese
Mix and pour over batter. Bake at 350 for 30 minutes Dust with powdered sugar

### LEMON SQUARES
*Brian, grandson*

Mix together:
3/4 cup butter
3 tbl sugar
1 and 1/2 cup flour

Pat into 9X12 pan. Bake 350 for 15 minutes.

4 eggs
2 tbl flour
2 cups sugar
1/2 cup lemon juice (best if you squeeze your own instead of using bottled juice)

Beat together in blender. Pour over crust. Return to the oven and bake another 15 minutes. When cooled, sprinkle with powdered sugar.

### CITRUS PUNCH
*Carolyn, granddaughter-in-law*

Combine:
3 cups orange juice
2 cups pineapple juice
1 quart lemonade
1 quart pitcher filled with ice water (primarily ice)

Add 1 quart ginger ale when ready to serve.

### FROZEN STRAWBERRY PIE
*Nikki, granddaughter*

8 oz cream cheese, softened
1 cup sugar
1 teaspoon vanilla
1 quart chopped fresh strawberries
1 carton (12 oz.) frozen whipped topping, thawed
1/2 cup chopped pecans
2 chocolate crumb crusts

In a large mixing bowl, beat the cream cheese, sugar and vanilla until smooth. Beat in the strawberries. Fold in the whipped topping and pecans. Pour into crusts. Cover and freeze 3-4 hours or until firm. Remove from freezer 10-15 minutes before serving. Serve with a dollop of whipped cream, a strawberry and chocolate curls.

*"I admit I am always the 'odd man out' as I don't like chocolate. However, that doesn't prevent me from enjoying all of the other sweet treats that are always in abundance at family get-togethers. Two of my favorites are gooey butter bars (these MUST be eaten frozen!) and lemon squares, two of grandma's and now Mom's often-used recipes."*

**Brian, grandson**

**CITRUS PUNCH**

*"We make Citrus Punch for our annual New Year's Eve party with the kids. It has been a tradition in the Zechmann family for generations. Easy and Healthy!"*

**Carolyn, granddaughter-in-law**

## CHRISTMAS CUT-OUT COOKIES
*Laura, granddaughter*
*(We usually double or triple this.)*

1 cup butter
2 eggs
1 cup sugar
1 teaspoon vanilla
2 1/2 cups flour
2 teaspoons baking powder
1 teaspoon cinnamon

I am sure there is a particular way to mix this together (wet ingredients/ dry ingredients), but we just basically follow the order and mix away. Refrigerate for an hour or two before rolling out to cut. Bake at 350 degrees for about 10 minutes (or more. We find that we like to cook them a little longer until really golden brown ... we just kind-of keep watch).

### FROSTING
After cooling we frost with a powdered sugar frosting:
1 stick of butter
2-4 cups of powdered sugar
1 teaspoon vanilla
milk for consistency

We mix and add until it looks (and tastes) good. Add food coloring and frost away!

## Tales from the Kitchen

One of my favorite memories is of making Christmas cookies. When I got married, I found that the Moynihan's love this tradition as well and that they use a recipe that has been handed down in their family for a long time. We've adopted it on the Henry side and even bring down cookie cutters and cooling racks to Florida in order to keep up the tradition each year.

**Laura, granddaughter**

## Whopper Pie
*Heather, granddaughter*

1/2 gallon vanilla ice cream
1/2 container Pet whip
Whoppers (crushed)
1 chocolate ready to use pie crust

Soften ice cream. Combine ice cream and whipped topping. Stir in 2/3 of the crushed Whoppers. Pour into pie shell. Spring top with remaining Whoppers. Freeze. When ready to serve, garnish with dabs of whipped topping and whole Whoppers. Drizzle with hot fudge sauce. Yield: 6-8 servings

**Note:** Any other candy can be substituted. Butterfingers also work well. But don't use the Oreo crust instead of chocolate. Chocolate is the way to go.

### Tips and Tricks
Do not miss any crevices or you'll be sorry. Trust me, I've been there.

**Edwina, granddaughter-in-law**

## Pecan Cream Cheese Brownies
*Kathy, granddaughter*

1 Box butter pecan cake mix
1 egg
1 stick butter

Mix and press in cake pan for the crust.

8 oz cream cheese
1 stick butter
2 eggs
1 lb powdered sugar

Mix until smooth, pour over crust. Bake at 350 for 55 minutes. Sprinkle 1 C of chopped pecans on top.

Pecan Cream Cheese Brownies

*"Move over, Thanksgiving pumpkin pie, Pumpkin Crunch is even better!"*

**Edwina,
granddaughter-in-law**

SHORTBREAD COOKIES

*"I make Shortbread Cookies for Hannah because it's one of the few egg-free cookies out there. But the real reason I make these cookies is because they perfume my kitchen with that captivating buttery-vanilla scent. I've burnt my chin (once as a teen cook and once as a thirty-something) trying to inhale as much of that intoxicating scent. There you have it, baking can be cause bodily injury."*

**Edwina,
granddaughter-in-law**

## PUMPKIN CRUNCH
*Edwina, granddaughter-in-law*

1 large can pumpkin
3 large eggs, beaten
1 cup sugar
1 teaspoon pumpkin pie spice (or mix ground cloves, cinnamon, ginger, nutmeg)
1 large can evaporated milk
1 box yellow cake mix (any brand, no pudding added)
1 cup chopped pecans or walnuts
1 cup butter, melted

### TOPPING
8 ounces cream cheese, softened
1 cup confectioner's sugar
1 teaspoon vanilla
1 regular tub Cool Whip

Prepare a 9x13 metal baking pan with non-stick cooking spray. Line the pan with parchment or wax paper, and set it aside. Preheat the oven to 350 degrees. In a large bowl, blend together the first 5 ingredients until combined well. Pour the pumpkin mixture into the prepared pan. Sprinkle all of the cake mix evenly over the pumpkin mixture. Liberally sprinkle the chopped nuts over the cake mix. Spoon the melted butter over the nuts and cake mix. Bake for one hour. Cool for 1 hour, and invert onto a serving platter. Frost with topping and refrigerate until ready to serve. To prepare the topping, cream the cheese with the sugar and vanilla until smooth. Fold in the Cool Whip until well blended.

## SHORTBREAD COOKIES
*Edwina, granddaughter-in-law*

1 cup butter (2 sticks)
1/2 cup sugar
1 tsp vanilla
2 cups flour

Preheat oven to 325 degrees. Line a 9x13 pan with foil. This makes for easy removal when cookies are done. Cream butter and sugar until light and fluffy. Add vanilla. Mix in flour. Press dough into the pan, and prick with fork. Bake for 35-40 minutes, or until light gold in color. Cut into squares while still warm.
**Option A**
Add 1/2 cup chopped nuts when you add the flour.
**Option B**
After you slice the cookies, place on a wire rack and drizzle with melted chocolate. To do this, place some chocolate chips into a ziptop bag. Microwave for 30 seconds or until chocolate is just melted. Snip the tip off with scissors, and go to town!
**Option C**
Follow option B, and sprinkle chopped nuts or chopped candy canes on top of the melted chocolate. That way, when the chocolate cools and hardens, the sprinkled stuff fuses with the chocolate. Chocolate will be your "glue" and your BFF.
**Note:** I like to double the recipe to yield a thicker cookie. The thicker the cookie, the softer it'll be. The thinner cookie, the more crispy.

## Tales from the Kitchen

If one were to ask any of the Henry grandkids what the words to "It's a Small World" were, I'll bet each of us could sing it word for word. It's a song that has a special place in my heart because it reminds me of the most magical place in the world, Disney World. Not only do the happy characters, wild rides, and amazing atmosphere make it a magical place but the memories I have from my childhood of being there with all of my cousins. Flying through the air on Dumbo, giving hugs to Mickey and Minnie at breakfast, running through the Polynesian village, making a trip around the world in Epcot, riding the Monorail, and even the plane ride to Florida when we looked  for the Care Bears on the clouds. I remember loving every minute of it and loving it even more because I got to be there with my whole family. The Henry family could have fun no matter where we were, but to be able to spend our childhood with our cousins, aunts, uncles, and grandparents in the "Happiest Place on Earth" is something I know we will never forget. The cousins still talk about the fun we had and laugh at pictures or fun stories in Disney. We were very blessed to have two wonderful people that were able and cared for us enough to take us there and make magical memories that will last a lifetime. Grandpa Merv and Grandma Helen started a tradition that my family has carried on, and that I hope to share with my kids and their cousins too.

**Kendi, granddaughter**

| | | |
|---|---|---|
| ADOBO | CARAMEL PECAN CINNAMON ROLLS | CREAMED TUNA |
| Edwina, granddaughter-in-law 57 | Jessie 47 | Helen 21 |
| AMERICAN PIZZA | CARAMEL PECAN PIE | CROCK POT BEANS |
| Helen 25 | Helen 45 | Brett, grandson 66 |
| APPLE CRISP | CATFISH, FRIED | |
| Helen 9 | Colleen, daughter 20 | DONUT BALLS |
| ASIAGO POTATO PUFFS | CHAMPAGNE PUNCH | Colleen, daughter 17 |
| Jeanne, daughter-in-law 14 | Colleen, daughter 19 | DOUBLE CHOCOLATE BROWNIES |
| AUGRATIN POTATOES | CHEESE FONDUE APPETIZERS | Jessie, daughter-in-law 32 |
| Helen 4 | Colleen, daughter 15 | EASY DONUTS |
| | CHEESE GARLIC BREADSTICKS | Colleen, daughter 16 |
| BACON HORSERADISH DIP | Jessie, daughter-in-law 18 | EGG CASSEROLE |
| Brett, grandson 49 | CHEESEY PEAS | Helen 11 |
| BANANA BREAD | Colleen, daughter 29 | EGG AND TUNA SCALLOP |
| Helen 13 | CHEESEY POTATOES | Helen 19 |
| BANANA BREAD | Colleen, daughter 28 | ELENI'S GREEK MARINADE |
| Lori, granddaughter 53 | CHERRY DUMP CAKE | Edwina, granddaughter-in-law 54 |
| BANANA SALAD | Colleen 40 | ENCHILADA ROLLS |
| Helen 10 | CHERRY PIE FILLING SALAD | Scott, grandson 57 |
| BASIC PIE CRUST (FOR ONE) | Helen 30 | ENGLISH TOFFEE |
| Helen 44 | CHICKEN & CHILIS | Maureen, daughter 47 |
| BEANY BURGERS | Michael A., grandson 55 | |
| Nikki, granddaughter 53 | CHICKEN AND NOODLES | FLATBREAD |
| BEEF STROGANOFF | Helen 24 | Brett, grandson 52 |
| Pat, daughter 24 | CHICKEN CHILI | FLUFFY WHITE CHOCOLATE CHIP MERINGUE BARS |
| BEER BATTER BREAD | Beth, granddaughter 59 | Kendi, granddaughter 69 |
| Jessie, daughter-in-law 18 | CHICKEN ENCHILADA QUICHE | FRUIT COCKTAIL CAKE |
| BLACK BEAN AND CORN SALSA | Nikki, granddaughter 56 | Helen 28 |
| Nikki, granddaughter 51 | CHICKEN PIE | FROZEN STRAWBERRY PIE |
| BLAKE'S FAVORITE PASTA BAKE | Megan, granddaughter-in-law 55 | Nikki, granddaughter 71 |
| Blake, grandson-in-law 62 | CHILLED PINEAPPLE BANANA DESSERT | |
| BLUEBERRY MUFFINS | Carolyn, granddaughter-in-law 70 | GERMAN CHOCOLATE CAKE |
| Jessie, daughter-in-law 17 | CHILI | Helen 40 |
| BLUEBERRY-SOUR CREAM BREAKFAST CAKE | Colleen, daughter 27 | GRAHAM STREUSEL CAKE |
| Edwina, granddaughter-in-law 67 | CHILI SUPREME | Pat, daughter 41 |
| BOILED POTATOES | Brittany, granddaughter-in-law 59 | GRILLED TURKEY STEAK |
| Helen 6 | CHINESE NEW YEAR COOKIES | Maureen, daughter 21 |
| BREAKFAST CASSEROLE | Helen 33 | GRANDMA'S LASAGNA |
| Jen R., granddaughter-in-law 68 | CHINESE NEW YEAR COOKIES | Heather, granddaughter 62 |
| BROCCOLI CHEESE SOUP | Joe, son-in-law 33 | GRASSHOPPERS |
| Pat, daughter 26 | CHIPPER CHICKEN | Colleen, daughter 19 |
| BROCCOLI CHEESE SOUP | Helen 8 | GREEN BEANS |
| Brittany, granddaughter-in-law 60 | CHOCOLATE CHIP COOKIES | Helen 29 |
| BROCCOLI RICE CASSEROLE | Maureen, daughter 34 | GOOEY BUTTER CAKE |
| Helen 27 | CHRISTMAS CUT-OUT COOKIES | Carole, granddaughter-in-law 70 |
| BROCCOLI RICE CASSEROLE | Laura, granddaughter 72 | GOULASH |
| Carole, daughter-in-law 66 | CITRUS PUNCH | Helen 24 |
| BROCCOLI SALAD | Carolyn, granddaughter-in-law 71 | |
| Helen (added by Laura, granddaughter) 28 | CLAM CHOWDER | HAM AND PEA TORTELLINI |
| BROWN GRAVY | Jeff, grandson 58 | Lori, granddaughter 61 |
| Helen 23 | COCO'S CRISPY CHICKEN | HAM AND POTATOE CASSEROLE |
| BROWNIE BAKED ALASKA | Colleen, daughter 22 | Helen 11 |
| Helen 41 | CONGO SQUARES | HAMBURGER CORN PIE |
| BRUSCHETTA | Helen 35 | Nikki, granddaughter 55 |
| Beth, granddaughter 51 | COTTAGE CHEESE FLUFF SALAD | HAMBURGER HASH |
| BUFFALO CHICKEN DIP | Helen 14 | Helen 20 |
| Beth, granddaughter 50 | CRAB MEAT DELIGHTS | HAMBURGER STEAKS |
| BUTTERSCOTCH BARS | Jessie, daughter-in-law 16 | Colleen, daughter 20 |
| Helen 32 | CREAM GRAVY | HAMBURGER STROGANOFF |
| BUTTERSCOTCH PIE | Colleen 22 | Helen 23 |
| Helen 3 | CREAM PIE | HAMLOAF |
| | Helen 5 | Helen 3 |
| CANDIED PECANS | CREAM PUFFS | HEARTY BISCUITS AND SAUSAGE GRAVY |
| Nikki, granddaughter 68 | Helen 36 | Greg, grandson 66 |

| Recipe | Contributor | Page |
|---|---|---|
| HOMEMADE ICE CREAM | Colleen, daughter | 42 |
| HOMEMADE MAPLE SYRUP | Helen | 10 |
| HOT CRAB DIP | Heather, granddaughter | 49 |
| HOT FUDGE SAUCE | Helen | 41 |
| ITALIAN BEEF | Pat, daughter | 20 |
| ITALIAN CHICKEN | Heidi, granddaughter-in-law | 53 |
| ITALIAN CHICKEN | Jen R., granddaughter-in-law | 54 |
| INDIVIDUAL CHEESECAKES | Maureen, daughter | 46 |
| JAMBALAYA | Mark, grandson | 61 |
| JIFFY FRUIT COBBLER | Joe, son-in-law | 40 |
| KATHY'S DIP | Kathy, granddaughter | 49 |
| LAYERED GREEN BEANS | Helen | 8 |
| LEMON SQUARES | Brian, grandson | 71 |
| LIME SHERBET | Kate, sister | 43 |
| LINGUINE CARBONARA | Pat, daughter | 25 |
| LOLA'S MARINADE | Edwina, granddaughter-in-law | 54 |
| LONG BOY CHEESEBURGERS | Mike and Angie, grandson and granddaughter-in-law | 56 |
| MADE RITE | Helen | 21 |
| MASHED POTATOES | Helen | 8 |
| MEAT LOAF | Colleen, daughter | 20 |
| MEAT SAUCE FOR SPAGHETTI | Cathy, granddaughter-in-law | 65 |
| MERRIGAN'S CHICKEN SALAD | Kristina, granddaughter | 65 |
| MICKEY PANCAKES | Kendi, granddaughter | 67 |
| MICROWAVE CARAMEL CORN | Jessie, daughter-in-law | 46 |
| MINT STUFF | Nancy, daughter | 43 |
| MISSISSIPPI MUD CAKE | Jessie, daughter-in-law | 38 |
| MOM'S ROLLS | Nancy, daughter | 16 |
| MONKEY BREAD | Amanda, granddaughter-in-law | 52 |
| NACHO DIP | The Tobin siblings, grandchildren | 50 |
| OAT AND CHOCOLATE BARS | Jessie, daughter-in-law | 32 |
| OATMEAL CAKE | Nancy, daughter | 37 |
| OREO DESSERT | Cathy, granddaughter-in-law | 69 |
| PAD THAI | Scott, grandson | 64 |
| PANCIT | Edwina, granddaughter-in-law | 63 |
| PASTA SALAD | Carole, granddaughter-in-law | 65 |
| PEANUT BUTTER BON BONS | Colleen, daughter | 45 |
| PEANUT BUTTER SAUCE | Nikki, granddaughter | 70 |
| PEANUT BUTTER FUDGE PIE | Pat, daughter | 45 |
| PECAN CREAM CHEESE BROWNIES | Kathy, granddaughter | 73 |
| PECAN PIE | Helen | 44 |
| PECAN SNOWBALLS | Helen | 31 |
| PECAN SURPRISE SQUARES | Helen | 7 |
| PUMPKIN CUPCAKES | Jessie, daughter-in-law | 37 |
| PUMPKIN CRUNCH | Edwina, granddaughter-in-law | 74 |
| PUMPKIN PIE CAKE | Helen | 39 |
| POT ROAST | Helen | 23 |
| PORCUPINES | Jessie, daughter-in-law | 21 |
| RYE BREAD DIP | Maureen, daughter | 15 |
| ROLO PRETZEL | Carolyn, granddaughter-in-law | 70 |
| RUM BALLS | Helen | 36 |
| SALMON PATTIES | Helen | 19 |
| SAN ANTONIO SALSA | Carolyn, granddaughter-in-law | 51 |
| SAUSAGE BALLS | Jessie, daughter-in-law | 16 |
| SAUSAGE QUICHE | Jessie, daughter-in-law | 27 |
| SCALLOPED PINAPPLE | Helen | 3 |
| SCOTT'S GRAND GUINNESS CHILI....BRILLIANT! | Scott, grandson | 58 |
| SCRUMPTIOUS BROWNIES | Jeanne, daughter-in-law | 32 |
| SHERRIED BEEF | Michael A., grandson | 53 |
| SHORTBREAD COOKIES | Edwina, granddaughter-in-law | 74 |
| SHRIMP SNACK | Colleen, daughter | 15 |
| SKILLET COOKIES | Helen | 31 |
| SOUR CREAM CHICKEN | Brett, grandson | 54 |
| SPAGHETTI SAUCE | Colleen, daughter | 25 |
| SPARTAN CHOCOLATE CHIP COOKIES | Nancy, daughter | 30 |
| SPINACH ARTICHOKE DIP | Nikki, granddaughter | 48 |
| SPINACH AND ARTICHOKE CASSEROLE | Jeanne, daughter-in-law | 28 |
| SPINACH BALLS | Helen | 15 |
| SPINACH/KRAUT SALAD | Mike and Angie, grandson and granddaughter-in-law | 66 |
| SPINACH LASAGNE | Carolyn, granddaughter-in-law | 63 |
| SPINACH WITH CHEESE | Colleen, daughter | 29 |
| SNICKERDOODLES | Colleen, daughter | 33 |
| STRAWBERRY CAKE | Helen | 39 |
| STRAWBERRY PIE | Helen | 44 |
| STRAWBERRY PIZZA | Jessie, daughter-in-law | 35 |
| STICKY CHINESE CHICKEN | Nikki, granddaughter | 54 |
| STIR IN THE PAN PIE CRUST | Jessie, daughter-in-law | 43 |
| STUFFED PORK CHOPS | Helen | 4 |
| SUGAR COOKIES | Helen | 31 |
| SWISS STEAK | Helen | 6 |
| TACO DIP | Brian, grandson | 49 |
| TACO SOUP | Cathy, granddaughter-in-law | 59 |
| TIM'S TASTY TUNA | Tim, grandson | 55 |
| TOMATO AND ZUCCHINI PASTA | Lori, granddaughter | 62 |
| TOMATO-BASIL SOUP | Kristina, granddaughter | 60 |
| TONY'S CHIPPED BEEF DIP | Tony, grandson | 50 |
| TUNA MACARONI | Colleen, daughter | 26 |
| TWICE BAKED POTATOES | Helen | 29 |
| VEGETABLE SOUP | Helen | 26 |
| WAFFLES | Helen | 10 |
| WHOPPER PIE | Heather, granddaughter | 73 |

Made in the USA